THE POLYANTHUS

FOR GARDEN, EXHIBITION
AND MARKET

By
ROY GENDERS

W. & G. FOYLE LTD.
119-125, CHARING CROSS ROAD, LONDON, W.C.2

First published 1958

© W. & G. FOYLE LTD.

Printed in Great Britain by
Liverpool Letterpress Limited, Liverpool and London

CONTENTS

1

THE POLYANTHUS—ITS ORIGIN

The origin of the polyanthus—Popularity of the Gold Laced polyanthus
—Miss Jekyll's Munstead strain—The modern polyanthus.

WHILST a number of the most popular florist's flowers of the
eighteenth and nineteenth centuries have, in modern times,
been pushed into the background, the polyanthus has never
been more popular than it is today. For so many years it
suffered in comparison with another member of the same
family, the Show auricula, and it came to be almost entirely
neglected, only the introduction of the modern post-war
strains having brought about its present popularity. Thomas
Hogg, in his famous Treatise of 1822, which deals with a
number of florist's flowers, devotes forty-seven pages to the
Show auricula yet only four to the polyanthus, and quite half
of the chapter is taken up with lists of varieties and the culture
of the double primrose. Thus, apart from the Gold Laced
polyanthus, the plant remained very much in the background
during the era of florist's flowers. Hogg mentions that 'the
most esteemed are a bright red, and a very dark crimson with
brimstone or lemon-coloured eyes and edging of the same',
this being of course the Gold Laced polyanthus, and he makes
no mention of any others.

Though the polyanthus as we know it is supposed to be
derived from a cross between the common primrose (*P. veris*)
and the cowslip (*P. vulgaris*) each in its wild form bears a
yellow flower, yet the first recorded instance of a plant similar
to that we know of as the polyanthus bore a red flower, on a
stem as long as that of the cowslip.

It was John Rea who wrote in his Flora of 1665 (in which
he also recorded the Black Imperial auricula): 'We now have
other kinds of primroses and cowslips that bear diversities of
red flowers . .'. the red cowslip or oxlip bearing many flowers
on one stalk, in fashion like those of the field, but of several red
colours'. It would appear from this that the polyanthus

similar to the plant we know today was then in cultivation, but exactly when the cross or first appearance took place we do not know. Like the Show auricula with the first appearance of the interesting paste-like centre, the appearance of the first polyanthus was never recorded, nor do we know by whom it was given the name 'polyanthos', from the Greek meaning 'many-flowered'. The same name has of more recent years been applied to most plants which bear a number of flowers in truss form on a single stem.

It would seem that red cowslips, which are now obtainable again, were known to Elizabethan gardeners and from these the first red polyanthus was evolved. The very many deviations of the primrose family has always ensured for this group of plants a special interest amongst gardeners. There are those which bear hose-in-hose flowers, one appearing inside another, and Jack-in-the-greens, the blooms being backed by an attractive green frill, and though borne on long polyanthus-like stems, several blooms appearing at the top, on short footstalks, these plants have never become well-known, nor does it appear that they have ever been used in the development of the modern polyanthus. It may, however, have been the polyanthus hose-in-hose to which Rea had referred, for Samuel Gilbert in his Florists' Vade Mecum of 1693 mentions 'Oxlips or Polyanthus's; I have very large hose-in-hose, of deeper or lighter reds'. From which it would appear that of several types of the primrose family the red colour was common to each, though we do not know how this came to be so.

In 1731, Philip Miller, a Scotsman living in London, published his famous Gardener's Dictionary in which he describes the 'Garden Polyanthus, with large red flowers' and mentions 'that there are a great variety at present in the gardens, such as the Hose-in-Hose, double Cowslip and all sorts of Polyanthus which have been so much improved during the past fifty years (from Gilbert's time) as to almost equal the variety of the auricula; and in some parts of England are so much esteemed as to sell for a guinea a root'.

POPULARITY OF THE GOLD LACED POLYANTHUS

By 1770 it is said that in the garden of Rev. William Hanbury in Leicestershire, there were over a 1,000 different kinds of polyanthus, and by the end of the century the plant had become well established as a florist's flower. M'Intosh, gardener to H. M. King of the Belgians, in *The Flower Garden* published in 1839, lists more than fifty famous varieties of that time, amongst the best being Waterhouse's, George IV and Archbishop of York. This was the well-known Sheffield florist who achieved fame in raising that fine Show auricula, Conqueror of Europe, the best variety of its day (1830-40). Thomas Hogg, writing at the same period, mentions Lee's Magnificent and Warriss's Alderman Wood as being amongst the best polyanthus of the time. He gives no description, but all were Gold Laced. This reveals that the famous auricula growers of the time were also turning their attentions to raising polyanthus, and by this time the Gold Laced polyanthus had made its appearance and become fully established.

One of the earliest enthusiasts of the laced polyanthus was the well-known Lancashire florist Samuel Barlow, who a century ago laid down certain standards defining a Gold Laced polyanthus of show quality, which have remained unaltered to the present day. It was the weavers of Lancashire and Yorkshire, who worked at home on their looms for long hours, who first appreciated these plants and it was they who set the standards of what constituted a top class flower. Unfortunately there is no record of where and to whom the first laced polyanthus appeared. There were also silver laced flowers, more rare than the golden and which now seem to have been entirely lost to cultivation.

The Gold Laced polyanthus first appeared on the show bench about the year 1800 or just before, and was widely grown until the late 1860's, when its popularity gradually declined until by the end of the century it was rarely seen, the more brilliantly coloured flowers, beloved by Victorian gardeners, having taken its place. It was one of the flowers included in "A Compot of Spring Flowers" published in Mrs. Loudon's *My Own Garden* in 1855, when the popularity of this charming flower was already on the wane. Happily, today there is renewed interest in the flower, the author having devoted many years in building up a strain which would stand comparison with the varieties of a century ago, when the Gold Laced polyanthus was thought fit to be included by James Maddock in his Florist's Directory together with such favourites as the hyacinth, ranunculus, carnation, tulip, pink, anemone and auricula. These were the flowers of the florists of the early nineteenth century, growers specialising in but one or two and growing them to perfection. Yet whilst the Gold Laced polyanthus was enjoying half a century or more of popularity, the ordinary polyanthus was being sadly neglected. Indeed, whilst the Show auricula and Gold Laced polyanthus were being brought to a state of near perfection, the ordinary polyanthus almost completely fell from favour until by 1875 it was, in most gardens but a memory.

MISS JEKYLL'S MUNSTEAD STRAIN

It was only by chance that an odd plant was found by Miss Gertrude Jekyll in 1880. From the seed she was to devote much of her long life in raising the famous Munstead strain of polyanthuses, and by the turn of the century the polyanthus was once again becoming a popular plant in the garden if not on the show bench. Yet as late as 1883, William Robinson wrote in *The English Flower Garden*, 'Polyanthuses are not at all sufficiently appreciated considering the wonderful array of beauty they present' and indeed it was not until a quarter of a century after Miss Jekyll's first hybridising that her Munstead strain achieved any great popularity. The first result of her hybridising was a yellow bloom of refined form and this was followed by a white polyanthus. These two predominated in the Munstead strain, with the result that the polyanthus lacked variety of colour and achieved only limited popularity. Still, Gertrude Jekyll's strain covered a wide range of golden yellow colourings and a white of great purity, and a start had been made to re-establish the polyanthus even if the new 'toy', the greenhouse and the more exotic plants which it could grow, was occupying most of the attentions of the Victorian gardener.

By the time the First World War had begun, a number of new colours had been introduced and these included cerise and crimson, nothing very exciting perhaps, yet their richer colouring was to bring the polyanthus a new popularity especially as a cut flower. During the years between the two wars, the plant became widely used for bedding and for planting in the less formal gardens, the size of bloom and length of stem continually being improved. The plant too, was becoming more widely grown in the West Country for its early bloom. This was finding a ready sale in the markets of the industrial North, the bloom being just right for the small town house. But those who could appreciate the polyanthus at that time would have been amazed at what might well be called the stupendous improvement of the bloom in the years following the Second World War.

THE MODERN POLYANTHUS

It was in 1950 that the new colours of the American polyanthus were first revealed to the author. In Cornwall, then growing anemones, I first came upon a small field of these superb plants when entering the tiny sea coast village of Coverack, down that rather steep winding hill. The time of the year was mid-February and a thick mist hung over the coast, as it so often does at this time of the year, yet the picture which lay before me was one that will never be forgotten. In spite of the mist, the plants, in full bloom, presented such brilliance of colouring that the field was as if planted with cinerarias rather than with polyanthuses, for until then only the familiar cerise, crimson, yellow and white blooms were known to me. Stopping the car on the hill, I made for the field and my eyes could scarcely take in the splendour. A lady, not the owner, picking violets alongside the strip of polyanthuses, told me that they were raised from American seed and could say no more. For two hours I remained gazing on their beauty. Most of the blooms were free of any eye or centre and were of every imaginable colouring, bright clear colours whose purity was accentuated by a lack of the usually too conspicuous centre. There were blooms of sky blue, slate grey, scarlet, terra-cotta, velvet crimson, peach tints and clear pinks. The usual cerise, white and yellow colours had been completely eliminated. Some fifty miles away in the Tamar Valley I informed a grower friend that although a prize winner each year for polyanthus at the Tamar Valley Show, held in March, I had seen plants which would create a sensation at the Show, and sure enough they did, taking First Prize.

This had been my first introduction to the famous American Barnhaven strain of polyanthuses, evolved by Mr. and Mrs. Levy and which must be classed with Peace rose, Bishop delphiniums and Russell lupins as amongst the finest and most valuable garden plants introduced during the century. For the past five years the beds of the American polyanthuses in my garden on the exposed North-East Coast have become a source of attraction to polyanthus lovers from all parts of Britain and those who have yet to grow the American strains cannot realise their magnificence. By dividing the plants each year after flowering, the few original plants have now become thousands and they remain as vigorous as ever. In a letter to the Secretary of the National Primula and Auricula Society, an American, Mr. Howard Lynn, himself the raiser of several magnificent strains of the polyanthus, says, 'the genius of Mrs. Florence Levy for plant breeding has made the Barnhaven strain the best that we have, and in most respects far better than anything the author has seen from Europe'. The huge trusses are borne on 18-inch stems, the individual florets measuring up to 3 inches across. Other famous American strains are those of the McHenrys, the Clarkes and the Tarpens each possessing a distinctive quality, whilst in the years prior to her recent death, Miss Linda Eickmann achieved considerable fame with her wonderful 'Crown Pink' strain. This charming lady succeeded after years of hybridising, of raising the first really clear pink-flowered polyanthus. It is in the moist climate of Oregon State that most of the American polyanthus enthusiasts grow their plants, though the strain which may be said to have formed the foundation of the modern American polyanthus originated at Cowichan Bay in British Columbia, the crimson-red flowers being free of any eye, whilst the foliage possessed the same rich bronzy-red tint of that of the Irish Garryarde primroses.

From New Zealand too, much has been done during post-war years to introduce a number of good strains though, having tried several in England, they do not seem to be the equal of several of the American strains.

At home, no one has done more to improve the polyanthus in post-war years than the famous Bath firm of Blackmore and Langdon. The great feature of their strains is the very large blooms, their rich colourings and compact habit, which make their polyanthus ideal for bedding. The Award of a Gold Medal by the Royal Horticultural Society for these polyanthus was well earned, for the strains rival the best of the American strains and have brought the polyanthus to near perfection. Other firms to have brought the polyanthus in Britian to a standard which could not have been conceived by Miss Jekyll or William Robinson are Sutton and Sons, Toogood's, and Clucas's in each of whose strains the old magenta and rather harsh yellow colourings have been almost entirely eliminated.

In his delightful book *Old Fashioned Flowers* (Country Life) Mr. Sacheverell Sitwell describes double polyanthuses such as Prince Silverwings and Curiosity, but with few exceptions I prefer to class these lovely plants as polyanthus-primroses for they are of more primrose habit and so most do not find a place in this book on the polyanthus. Most of the doubles differ from the true polyanthus in that the large double blooms are borne on footstalks almost as long and often longer than the main stem which is generally no more than 2 inches in length, and so these glorious old world plants should be classed with the double primroses such as Quaker's Bonnet and *alba plena* which are of the true primrose habit. There are, however, several of the doubles which are of true polyanthus form, most of them being extremely rare.

The miniature polyanthuses, which have the same habit as their more robust cousins and which must surely become just as popular in the coming years, and several bearing hose-in-hose flowers borne on 12-inch stems, may also be classed as of true polyanthus habit. Each of these prove charming subjects for window box culture whilst they also carry the delicious woodland fragrance of the primrose. During the next decade many more lovely polyanthuses are certain to be introduced and all the time the famous breeders are working to improve existing strains. Miss Eickmann's pure pink and the pure marine blues have now become almost fixed so that they may be relied upon to reproduce themselves from seed with very little deviation in colour, whilst most strains have now eliminated that undesirable magenta and cerise shades and many of the rather too common yellow colours. It has, however, taken the polyanthus 250 years to attain its present form and popularity, but it now seems to have established itself throughout the Western world in the same way as has the rose and chrysanthemum. Perhaps more so, for with the modern small suburban garden replacing the large garden of the country house and the ever-rising cost of fuel making a greenhouse too great a luxury for most plant lovers, the hardy and reliable polyanthus becomes more popular each year. It is now estimated that more than ten million plants are sold in America each year, and almost the same number in Great Britain, for with its freedom from pest and disease, its cleanliness and value both as a cut flower and for garden decoration there are few plants its equal.

2

MODERN POLYANTHUS STRAINS.
FOR BEDDING, CUTTING AND EXHIBITION

Polyanthus Strains

AMERICAN WINE RED. Extremely robust, the large almost black blooms being held on 18-inch stems, the yellow eye being almost completely absent. I believe this strain was introduced by the McHenry's but would not be quite certain of this. It is a strong grower in Britain.

BLUE STRAINS. Quite excellent is Blackmore and Langdon's strain, the blooms being large, with a conspicuous yellow centre, the colours ranging from dark purple-blue to palest sky blue, the paler colours being more attractive. The American Marine Blue strain raised by the Barnhaven Gardens from G. F. Wilson's original blue stock has possibly not so sturdy a habit, neither is the bloom quite so large, but the colour is fixed somewhere between sky and china blue. The blooms possessing that attractive smoky sheen which places the American polyanthus in a class to itself, whilst the bloom is quite free from the red and purple colouring which spoils so many blue strains.

BRILLIANCY. This strain is excellent for cutting, the trusses being borne on long, wiry stems and whilst the individual pips are not large they are of the most vivid colourings imaginable; terra-cotta, tangerine, rust and orange being represented, whilst all other colours have been eliminated. One of the brightest flowers of the garden, and excellent for cloche culture. Introduced by Messrs. Sutton & Sons.

BROADWELL STRAIN. The clear colours of the blooms and the fact that the yellow centre does not smudge into the

13

petal colour makes this strain one of the best of those raised in Britain. The individual blooms measure almost 2 inches across and are of the richest colourings, the scarlets, maroons, crimsons and purples which predominate, possessing a striking velvety sheen. Whites, yellows and magentas have almost been eliminated.

CLUSEED BLYTHE MAXIMUM STRAIN. Evolved by Messrs. J. L. Clucas Ltd., this is one of the finest of the British strains, especially for cutting. The blooms, which are borne on long, wiry-stems measure between 2-3 inches across and are chiefly of the red shades which include pale pink, rose, scarlet, crimson and maroon as well as a number of pink pastel shades such as peach-pink.

COLOSSAL STRAIN. Evolved by the Clarkes in America, this strain lives up to the very high standards set by the American growers. The blooms are very large and many are two coloured such as cream shading to pink, and petals of gold and red rather like Masquerade rose. Burgundy, fuchsia-pink, salmon and peach are also included in the mixture.

COLOSSEA STRAIN. Raised in Holland, this is one of the most free flowering of all and though the blooms are extremely large, the colour range would be improved if the yellows and magentas were eliminated.

COWICHAN STRAIN. As previously mentioned, this strain was evolved from a plant obtained from British Columbia, conspicuous by its complete lack of eye. From this a strain has been raised by the Barnhaven Gardens comprising the most exciting shades of smoky red, garnet, amethyst, yes, even smouldering violet-grey, accentuated by the complete lack of any eye.

CRIMSON KING. There is almost no difference between the true strain and the Ipswich Giant Crimson strain raised by Messrs. Thompson and Morgan Ltd. Both are excellent for garden decoration and for cutting, the individual blooms being large and borne in trusses of fifteen or more pips. The colour is richest velvety crimson with a conspicuous, but small golden eye.

CROWN PINK. This beautiful strain was introduced by Miss Linda Eickmann shortly before her death in 1956, and is the first real pink strain to give any degree of uniformity. The colour is clearest pink without any trace of rose or salmon. Whilst not quite so robust as most polyanthuses, the blooms are large and well formed. Miss Eickmann introduced a number of named pinks from her strain such as Warm Laughter and Radiance.

DEEP ORANGE STRAIN. This is a new strain introduced by Carter's Ltd., and owing to its brightness is extremely valuable for shady bedding. The habit is compact, the vivid orange colouring coming almost 100% true from seed.

DESERT SUNSET STRAIN. A Barnhaven introduction of great beauty. The blooms are large and are borne in huge trusses on 15-inch stems, the pastel colourings ranging from coral-pink to creamy apricot, from peach to copper, from beige to tangerine-orange and possessing that remarkable smoky-velvet sheen.

GIANT BOUQUET STRAIN. Raised by Messrs. Watkin and Simpson Ltd., the plants are extremely free flowering, the trusses generally numbering twenty or more blooms. The colours, which are clean and bright, include violet, pale lilac, bronze, cream and crimson.

GOLDEN QUEEN. Raised by Messrs. Blackmore and Langdon, the blooms are of rich saffron yellow and come remarkably true to colour. The trusses, borne on 12-inch stems, are quite huge, often composed of two dozen or more blooms which makes this an ideal strain for bedding.

GOLD MEDAL STRAIN. The speciality of Messrs. Blackmore and Langdon, and quite outstanding. The blooms are often up to 3 inches across and comprise white, gold, blue, pink, bronze and flame colours, which may also be obtained separately. Blackmore and Langdon's Flame is possibly the richest coloured polyanthus in cultivation. The habit is sturdy, the stems being short and thick, making this an outstanding strain for bedding.

HOOD RIVER STRAIN. Like all the American strains, this embraces the most unusual smoky colours as well as primrose yellow, peach-pink and blue. The stems are compact, the blooms of medium size making it ideal for window boxes. The author is not certain of the raisers.

KELMSCOTT STRAIN. Introduced by Messrs. Harrison and Sons, this is a superb strain, the trusses being extremely large whilst the blooms are of every colour imaginable. The individual blooms are large and beautifully formed.

KWAN YIN. This Barnhaven strain is unsurpassed for the richness of its blooms which are large, almost without any eye, and embrace such remarkable shades as crushed tomato, Chinese red, cherry, scarlet, tile red, all indescribably brilliant with the sun on them. The strain, contrary to certain opinions, is quite as hardy as all British strains and is ideal for cutting.

MINIATURES. These delightfully dainty plants have been raised by the Barnhaven Gardens from crossing the ordinary polyanthus with the stalked-forms of the primrose-polyanthus. The blooms are slightly larger than the stalked primroses like Lady Greer which has been used in the breeding of the miniatures, whilst the stems are about 1 inch longer and somewhat thicker. One of the first and best of the miniatures to appear was Red Riddle, raised by Dr. Matthew Riddle of New York. Its dainty form and the glowing ruby red colour of the blooms made it a favourite from the beginning.

MUNSTEAD STRAIN. By far the best strain of Miss Jekyll's original Munstead polyanthuses is that marketed by Messrs. Carter's Ltd., who during recent years have improved upon it out of all recognition to that of fifty years ago. Though the colour range is comprised of only the original white and yellow tones, new oranges and pale yellows and much larger blooms now make this a most attractive strain, especially for planting in shaded positions where the more sombre colourings would not be shown to advantage.

PACIFIC STRAIN. Raised in California by Messrs. Vetterle and Reinelt of delphinium fame, the colour range is extremely wide, embracing blues, pinks, crimsons and pastel shades with a large golden centre. The plants are extremely free flowering but as their place of introduction would suggest, they have not quite the extreme hardiness of the East Coast American strains.

READ'S FESTIVAL STRAIN. This is a reliable strain for cutting, for the blooms are held on stems of at least 18 inches long, and include a wide range of colours in which shades of pink, rose and crimson predominate. The trusses are large and freely produced.

SNOW WHITE. Raised by Messrs. Blackmore and Langdon, this is one of the best of the white strains, the blooms being large with a conspicuous small orange eye, the petals being attractively frilled.

SPETCHLEY STRAIN. This strain, introduced by Messrs. Wallace and Barr, is extremely valuable for cutting, the colour range being wide, the trusses large, the stems long.

SUNSET HYBRIDS. Raised by Messrs. Carter's Ltd., this strain may be classed as the bedding counterpart of Sutton's Brilliancy strain. The colour range is similar and includes tangerine, buff and amber shades, whilst the large trusses are held on sturdy 9-inch stems.

SUTTON'S FANCY. This is one of the finest strains for bedding, for like the strains of Blackmore and Langdon, the individual blooms or pips are very large, the truss being flat and compact with the stems 9-10 inches in length. The full beauty of the blooms are thus clearly revealed. The stems are extremely thick to withstand adverse weather, whilst the colour range includes chiefly the art or pastel shades of peach, pink, apricot, lilac and cream.

SUTTON'S SUPERB. Whilst the Fancy strain is composed chiefly of pastel shades, the Superb strain is made up of more brilliant colourings, particularly bronzes, maroons and orange tints, the habit being similar to that of the Fancy strain and so making it very suitable for bedding.

TANGO SUPREME. This is one of the famous New Zealand strains raised by Messrs. Harrisons. The plants have a vigorous habit and bear a large truss of bloom, the individual pips measuring up to 3 inches across. The colour range includes oranges, bronzy-golds, buffs and vermilion. A pink strain, also evolved by Harrisons is of interest, many of the blooms being two-coloured, such as pink and cream, peach and white.

TOOGOOD'S GIANT EXCELSIOR STRAIN. The large flower trusses are held on 10- to 12-inch stems and so are ideal for cutting or bedding though preferably for the latter purpose. The colour range includes most of the pastel shades of apricot, peach, pink and cream, the magentas having been eliminated.

VICTORIAN STRAIN. The colour range is most ususual comprising smoky violet, smoke-grey, blackberry, mulberry, plum, lavender and purple, which are even more attractive when mixed with plants of the Kwan Yin strain. This is also a Barnhaven introduction and extremely beautiful.

Named Single Polyanthuses

There are a number of polyanthuses which may be the result of a primrose-polyanthus cross, but which because of their long stalk and the formation of a compact flower truss may be classed as of true polyanthus habit. The blooms of each are somewhat daintier than those of the modern polyanthus strains and the plants are of more compact habit. With their intensely rich colouring they are amongst the most attractive of all garden plants. All possess extreme hardiness, whilst they are very free flowering.

BARROWBY GEM. With Beltany Red, this is one of the finest of all spring plants, ideal for window box or rockery with its sturdy habit. It was raised in Scotland and is now rarely seen, though in the author's garden are several hundred plants of great vigour. It is the first polyanthus to come into bloom, the first pips opening on a mild February day, whilst its large umbrella like heads remain colourful until June. The bloom may be described as primrose yellow shaded green and it carries a pleasant almond perfume.

BARTIMEUS. This is believed to be a polyanthus of eighteenth century days. It bears a bloom of velvety crimson-black and has no eye. In its place is a region of bronzy-red. The blooms are not large nor does it form a large head in comparison with modern standards. This is the old Eyeless polyanthus, a connoisseur's plant.

BELTANY RED. Its origin is unknown, but it is one of the finest of all garden plants. It forms a stocky, compact plant and bears a large truss of tangerine-red blooms, which have an unusual green centre and an attractive wire-edge of gold. The leaves are vivid green. The plant remains ten weeks in bloom, and two or three planted together can be seen from afar.

FAIR MAID. The author obtained this magnificent variety from Perthshire, so it is well named. The small, but beautifully rounded blooms, are freely produced on numerous 15-inch stems, their colour being burnt orange-scarlet with a most striking double centre of gold. The blooms remain fresh in water for fully two weeks.

HUNTER'S MOON. A modern polyanthus and a beauty, for like Barrowby Gem it comes into bloom before all others and carries a fragrance the equal of Ena Harkness rose. Of sturdy habit, the bloom is of a lovely shade of apricot with a chrome yellow centre.

IDEAL. The small blooms are of a rich shade of paeony-purple and have a bright yellow eye, each petal being flecked with white. Of robust habit, the blooms are held on 10-inch stems and are freely produced.

KINLOUGH BEAUTY. Like all the named polyanthuses, this native of Scotland bears masses of small blooms of a warm shade of salmon-pink with a white candy stripe down each petal. Extremely free flowering and hardy.

LADY GREER. A most dainty polyanthus and a charming plant for a window box or trough garden. The tiny pale yellow blooms are held on 8- to 9-inch stems above attractively rounded bottle green foliage. This variety is being widely used in America for crossing.

PRINCE ALBERT. Another old polyanthus, the blooms being small and borne in clusters rather than in trusses. The bloom is of a crimson-plum colour, with a blush-blue candy stripe down the edge of each petal. Not of so robust habit as the others.

SPRING DARLING. The blooms are small, but borne in profusion on 15-inch stems and are of a rich cherry-red colour. Raised in Holland and a most vigorous grower.

Gold Laced

This interesting old polyanthus bears a bloom which has a golden centre, a red or black ground with gold lacing round the petals. The body or ground colour is generally of black, crimson, red or intermediate shades, and there has never appeared a laced polyanthus having a ground of any other colour apart from shades of red in varying degrees of intensity. The old named varieties have almost entirely disappeared, though with a revival of interest new varieties are almost certain to appear in the next decade. One of the finest strains is that marketed by Messrs. Nutting and Sons Ltd. Like all the Golden Laced polyanthuses, the blooms are not large, no more than 1 inch across, but are borne in trusses of a dozen or more on 12- to 15-inch stems. The ground colour of the new strains is of various shades of velvety-red, whilst the lacing is remarkably good. The author is at present working on a special strain of the Gold Laced polyanthus using the Nutting strain and several others from America as parents. The blooms are rather larger than the parent strains, have a deep crimson body colour and a well defined centre and golden-yellow lacing.

Another excellent strain is that introduced by Lew and Florence Levy at Barnhaven, the lacing being rather wider than that of the English strains, whilst the body colour is rich mahogany-red and remarkably consistent.

Double Polyanthuses

There are a number of these old-fashioned plants which bear their bloom trusses on long stems and which may be classed as being of the true polyanthus order. Most of them are extremely difficult to obtain and require a richer soil than all other members of the family. Particularly do the plants require liberal quantities of nitrogen of an organic nature, thoroughly decayed farmyard manure being most suitable.

ARTHUR DE SMIT. Raised in Belgium and thought to be now extinct, this was a beautiful variety, the bright purple flowers being edged with yellow.

CHEVITHORNE PINK. A charming variety which bears small, button-like blooms on short, sturdy stems. The blooms are of a lovely shade of shell pink, and contain much primrose 'blood'.

CRIMSON EMPEROR. A very rare variety but a vigorous grower, the large fully double blooms being of a bright crimson-red colour.

CRIMSON KING. Thought to be the Old Scottish Red double polyanthus, it is of less polyanthus habit than Crimson Emperor. The large blooms are of rich rosy-red.

CURIOSITY. Also known as Golden Pheasant and Tortoishell, this old variety is now very rare. The blooms are of an interesting combination of cherry, scarlet, pink and gold, as if splashed on with a paint brush.

PRINCE SILVERWINGS. May be said to be a semi-double, it is the only double polyanthus to bear pollen. The blooms are of a rich mulberry shade, flecked with brown and edged with white and with an orange blotch at the base of each petal.

ROSE OF SHERWOOD. Raised in Scotland, this is a fine new double polyanthus of great vigour and bearing large blooms of bright cerise-red.

Hose-in-Hose Polyanthus

There are a number of beautiful hose-in-hose polyanthuses, so named because of their likeness to the hose of Tudor days, one stocking being carried to the knees and over another which extends to the thighs. With their dainty habit they are amongst the loveliest plants of the garden and are very long lasting in water.

ALABASTER. Not quite as tall growing or as robust as the others mentioned here, but of more polyanthus than of primrose habit. The blooms are pure white with a yellow centre.

ASHFORD. A very old variety having long, rounded leaves and bearing flowers of rich reddish-brown which are held on 12-inch stems.

BRIMSTONE. A new introduction, the beautifully formed bell-like flowers being of a pure shade of brimstone-yellow.

DUSKY MAID. A magnificent variety of extremely vigorous habit, the large dusky plum-red blooms being held on 10-inch stems.

GOLDILOCKS. The dazzling yellow blooms are borne on 13-inch stems and remain colourful right through spring and early summer.

IRISH SPARKLER. A native of Ireland and a most striking variety, the tiny blooms, one inside another, are of a vivid orange-scarlet colour with an equally brilliant golden centre. Also known as Old Vivid.

Jack-in-the-Green Polyanthus

Just as there are hose-in-hose polyanthus as well as hose-in-hose primroses, so also there are Jack-in-the-Green forms of both. Here, the bloom is backed or surrounded by a large green ruff in the form of small leaves which greatly adds to the appearance of the bloom. When the bloom dies back, the green ruff persists for several weeks and so they are delightful for mixing with ordinary polyanthus blooms for indoor decoration. The polyanthus Jacks are borne on sturdy stems 10-12 inches long, the blooms being large with the ruff in proportion. They are obtainable in shades of red, crimson-brown, rose, yellow and white, the latter being the most rare and the most beautiful with its bloom of glistening white backed by its ruff of bottle green. There are also a number of wonderful named varieties:—

ELDORADO. This is a magnificent plant, the large, clear golden-yellow bloom being backed by a large rich green ruff and held on sturdy 10-inch stems.

SALAMANDER. This old Jack bears the largest bloom of any known polyanthus, measuring more than 3 inches across and more than 4 inches if the ruff is taken into account. The colour is brightest crimson-red with a large, clearly defined star-shaped centre.

Cowslip

As it is from the wild cowslip that our modern polyanthus is descended, this lovely old-fashioned flower must be remembered here. During post-war years Messrs. Unwins have produced a magnificent strain known as Unwin's Hybrids, which are worthy of growing beside the finest polyanthus strains. The dainty cupped blooms are borne in profusion on long 15-inch stems and embrace all the best colours of the modern polyanthus, including chestnut, bronze, amber, biscuit, maroon, smoked salmon, lilac and chrome-yellow. Of extremely vigorous habit, the plants soon form large clumps and send up an abundance of flower stems which are ideal either for cutting or for bedding.

3

THE POLYANTHUS IN THE GARDEN

JUST as the primrose and cowslip have always been the favourite flower of the children, so the polyanthus is now one of the most popular flowers of the garden. Shakespeare frequently mentioned the cowslip, for the polyanthus was not then known. Milton too, and John Clare, that lovely poet, also had the cowslip close at heart when writing their poetry, but the first mention of the polyanthus by a poet of renown was by John Thomson in his poem *Spring*, written in 1740 when the polyanthus was then just becoming known to gardeners.

'Polyanthus of unnumbered dyes' he wrote, which clearly shows that by then the polyanthus was to be obtained in numerous colours. But it was John Clare who in his poem Cowslips and Primroses, reveals the true characteristics of the family.

> 'The cottager when coming home from plough
> Brings home a cowslip root in flower to set'.

This being one of the chief characteristics of the family in that the plants may be removed when in full bloom and may be replanted with but little detriment to the bloom. In other words, the plants may be moved at almost any time of the year. Again Clare writes of 'their crimpled, curdled leaves' which the primrose, polyanthus and cowslip have been endowed by nature, from the surface of which every drop of moisture is directed along the many channels to the crown of the plant and to its roots. The plants are thus able to obtain sufficient moisture from the atmosphere at night-time during the warmer periods of the year and especially during late springtime when the plants are in full bloom, and which is generally the driest period of the year. To enable this natural irrigation system to be entirely efficient, all the leaves are borne from the crown at ground level so that no moisture is lost on its way to the roots. The fleshy roots too, enable them to store up moisture to a greater extent than would more fibrous roots.

REQUIREMENTS OF THE PLANT

The polyanthus being the result of a cross between the primrose and cowslip may be said to have taken on the characteristics of both plants. It requires an abundance of moisture at its roots during the summer months and whilst it will flourish in shade, it is happiest in the words of Thomas Hogg, 'in a situation exposed to the morning rays of the sun and excluded from them for the rest of the day'. Here again in choice of situation the polyanthus may be said to come halfway between the primrose and cowslip, the former appreciating dappled shade, the latter a position of full sun. The primrose is a flower of the hedgerow, the cowslip of the open meadow especially where low lying, to enable it to receive sufficient moisture. Provided the plants are given an abundance of humus about the roots, the polyanthus will be quite happy in full sun for in such a situation are the plants set out by the cut flower growers of Cornwall. Where a garden is exposed to the direct rays of the sun, the polyanthus may be grown to the same perfection as where grown in shade, though as Thomas Hogg has mentioned, shelter from the mid-day sun will prevent the blooms from fading and will ensure an extended flowering season. Where given a position of full shade, possibly beneath tall trees, though the display will be prolonged, the full richness of colouring will not be revealed and much of the beauty of the modern polyanthus will be lost. The plants, however, will tolerate full shade possibly better than any other plant and so may be planted on the shaded or northern side of a building where few other plants would bloom well, or beneath mature trees whose shade would be detrimental to the flowering of most plants. Where planting in such a position, it is important to ensure that adequate supplies of moisture reach the roots, for mature trees tend to deprive the soil of moisture for a considerable radius. For the same reason, where polyanthuses are planted in a shrubbery, the soil should first be thoroughly enriched with humus-forming manures. All too often because the plants will tolerate shade they are planted in impoverished soil, with the result that they never bloom as well as they may be expected. Planting beneath tall trees will also mean that the plants will be deprived of rain and dew which, in the smallest quantity, they can utilise to good advantage throughout the spring and summer. The plants, however, will be happy in the dappled shade of a young orchard or planted amongst young ornamental trees. Here the sparseness of top foliage will enable natural moisture to reach the plants, whilst they will receive valuable protection from the hot summer sun.

A young orchard is the ideal place in which to grow on the plants during summer after they have finished flowering in the beds, when they must be divided and replanted into a humus-laden soil and kept well watered until the new roots have formed. Or a northerly aspect, possibly beneath a wall, will prove suitable. The plants may, of course, be left in their flowering quarters and interplanted with summer bedding plants which will provide almost all the protection from the summer sun the plants require. The cut flower grower will generally lift, divide and replant where the plants are to bloom the following spring. The value of the polyanthus is that it multiplies rapidly, a single plant forming three or four crowns or offsets each year, which makes it essential that it should be divided at least every alternate year. The plants also come quickly into bloom. From a mid-summer sowing, the plants will come into bloom in March and will continue until early June, a period of at least ten weeks. No heat is required to raise the polyanthus and no glass covering is necessary for the plants to come into bloom early in spring. Nor is the plant particular as to soil, provided it is enriched with humus to enable it to retain summer moisture, and is reasonably well drained in winter.

THE HARDINESS OF THE POLYANTHUS

The polyanthus is one of the hardiest and most perennial plants of the garden, for it grows well in Northern Canada, in temperatures below zero, and is well able to withstand the coldest of English winters. It may be expected to bloom to perfection in the north of Scotland exactly as it does at the southernmost part of Cornwall, only the flowering times being different. So tough is the plant, and that word seems to be most suitable to use for the polyanthus, that the author, on moving homes, was forced to place in storage along with his furniture, the whole of his large collection of primrose and polyanthus plants. There they remained for eight weeks in tea chests entirely without attention until they could be replanted in November. The following spring every plant covered itself in bloom as if the disturbance had never taken place.

Where cold winds make it difficult to grow the wallflower and Brompton stock to perfection and where they may be experienced in a coastal garden or one unduly exposed, the polyanthus should be grown instead. Likewise where hard frosts may prove troublesome where the garden is low lying, the polyanthus is well able to survive where most other plants would give a poor account of themselves.

Being extremely sturdy in flowering, no artificial protection will be necessary, though where unduly exposed the plants will appreciate 9-inch boards placed around them on the sides of the prevailing winds. This will help them to bloom earlier and will prevent any 'burning' of the young foliage in March when cold winds are most troublesome. Short branches of privet or other evergreens may be used in place of the boarding, and where the ground is unduly exposed it will be advisable to plant those strains and varieties of short, compact habit.

THE POLYANTHUS FOR BEDDING

Where growing for bedding, and the polyanthus is invaluable for bridging the gap between the main bulb display and the first of the herbaceous or summer bedding flowers, the plants should be massed to obtain the best effect, planting 12 inches apart in slightly raised beds, or several inches wider where the plants are to be left in the beds throughout the year and interplanted with summer flowering plants. Eliminating much labour, this method has much to recommend itself in the present day garden where labour and time are at a premium. It will be necessary to plant only into thoroughly clean ground and to enrich the soil with humus so that the plants may be left undisturbed for possibly as long as two years. Summer flowering plants may be set out between the polyanthus plants, the less hardy annuals and other plants a fortnight earlier than normally, for they will receive valuable protection from the polyanthus plants, whilst the hardier plants may also be planted out earlier than would

be the case where it is necessary to wait for the polyanthuses
to finish flowering. Altogether inter-planting is a most satisfactory method of bedding under modern conditions.

To plant with the polyanthus for a spring display, the
myosotis (forget-me-not) is excellent, using a variety which
is of dwarf habit. Plant the dwarf strain of Sutton's Royal
Blue which grows only 6 inches tall, or the attractive
Wraysbury Blue of similar habit, the bright blue flowers
having a conspicuous yellow eye. With the myosotis use
polyanthuses of yellow and orange shades, or reverse the
colourings and with the blue flowered polyanthus, plant the
Winter or Perpetual flowering pansies which are at their best
during spring and early summer. The yellow Helios or the
white Snowstorm will provide contrasting colours. Or use
the purple pansy March Beauty to carpet a bed of Sutton's
Brilliancy polyanthus, or Snowstorm to carpet a bed of
Crimson King or Blackmore and Langdon's Flame polyanthus, planted 15 inches apart. If the bed is made up towards
the end of October and the soil has been well enriched with
humus, the plants may be left undisturbed for eighteen months,
flowering through two successive spring periods. The blue
polyanthus is also most attractive used with the dwarf Golden
Bedder wallflower which grows to the same height as the
polyanthus. The wallflower plants will receive valuable
protection from the polyanthus leaves during early spring.

For very small beds, the double daisies, *Bellis perennis*
are charming plants for carpeting a bed of polyanthuses.
The dainty salmon-pink flowered Dresden China brightens up
a bed of blue or crimson polyanthuses; its white counterpart
may also be used, whilst the crimson-red Rob Roy makes an
attractive carpet to white polyanthus plants. Most attractive
is the white double daisy planted between Gold Laced
polyanthus, their rich crimson and gold colouring providing
a striking contrast.

Though beds of mixed polyanthuses are most frequently
seen, quite delightful displays may be arranged by using
selected colours. The beds may be of circular or rectangular
shape, and should be slightly raised so that the plants at the
centre will reveal their full beauty. Also it will be advisable to
use those with longer stems to the centre of the bed. A striking
display may be obtained by planting circles of double rows of
crimson or flame, white, and blue; or a rectangular bed

planted with pink polyanthuses at the centre and surrounded by the American pale blues will look most attractive. Where the beds are to be made in shade, use should be made of the brighter colours, the yellow and orange shades, the flame coloured varieties such as Beltany Red, the white, and the peach and pink colours. The darker coloured flowers should be confined to the sunnier, more open situations.

Where planting in rows along a path or entrance drive, three rows of different colours will give a striking display, those bearing their bloom on taller stems being planted to the rear. Crimson King at the back, Desert Sunset colours to the middle, with Lady Greer to the front will give a 'bank' of rich colouring. Or use Brilliancy at the back, Blackmore and Langdon's Blues in the middle and the Cowichan strain to the front for an equally rich effect. Given a soil rich in humus and an annual mulching with peat or leaf mould after flowering, the plants may remain undisturbed for three years. It must also be remembered that modern polyanthuses with their long, sturdy stems are valuable flowers for cutting in addition to their bedding qualities, and a bed in full bloom will provide plenty of flowers for the home.

For the very small garden, the 'miniatures' should be planted and here could be included the dainty, small flowering Fair Maid and Lady Greer. A charming bed may be made up by planting Fair Maid or Beltany Red at the centre and surrounding them with Lady Greer. For small beds about an entrance to a house, polyanthus may be planted permanently 16-18 inches apart and for spring display, daffodils or dwarf tulips may be planted either directly in the bed or may be introduced in pots when in bud. The large trumpet daffodils of not too tall a habit and especially the pure whites Beersheba or Mount Hood, are lovely when set in pots between blue, flame or crimson polyanthuses. The double dwarf tulips, such as the yellow Van der Hoef and Marechal Niel are also most attractive planted between blue or crimson polyanthuses, or use the pure white Snow Queen with Gold Laced polyanthuses or those of the Barnhaven Victorian strain. A striking and inexpensive combination is the Golden Queen polyanthus with the fiery red tulip, Orange Nassau which grows to the same height.

For a heavenly perfume plant a small bed of the greenish-yellow, almond-scented Barrowby Gem with the violet-scented

Iris reticulata, both coming into bloom in the coldest garden
well before the end of March.

Where bulbs are favoured for late spring bedding, the
blue hyacinth Myosotis is most attractive planted with the
yellow and orange polyanthuses, or with pink strains. Or
use the crimson flowered Jan Bos with white polyanthuses. So
much more may be done with polyanthuses of separate
colours and varieties than with merely planting mixed strains,
many of which do not include modern colours. Remember too,
that the polyanthus is one of the most permanent plants of the
garden. Unlike those which are widely used for spring bedding,
and which are of biennial habit, the polyanthus is fully
perennial and provided it is given good culture the plants
should remain healthy for many years. With its habit of
dying back each winter when only one or two leaves remain,
the plant is little troubled by town conditions, where deposits
of soot and sulphur cause trouble to many plants, for new
foliage appears each year at the beginning of spring when
winter fogs will almost have disappeared. No plant is more
tolerant of town conditions and it is adverse soil conditions
rather than smoke deposits which may occasionally trouble
the plants, for the soil of city gardens is all too frequently dry
and lifeless. Cold winds, torrential rains, severe frost or strong
sunshine will have little effect on the polyanthus provided the
soil is well drained and is well supplied with humus.

When the plants remain in the beds after flowering, they
may be inter-planted with plants to bloom from early June
until the autumn when they are then removed and the
polyanthuses are again inter-planted with plants or bulbs to
bloom in spring. For a summer display, nemesia, antirrhinums,
stocks, asters, salvias and almost all plants which bloom at a
height of from 12-18 inches will be suitable, for they will hide
the polyanthus foliage almost entirely, whilst the dead flower
stems will have been removed. By setting out the summer
flowering plants early in May, whilst the polyanthuses are
in full bloom, there will be little or no break in the display,
whereas five or six weeks will elapse if it is necessary to wait
until the polyanthus display has ended and the plants lifted
before bedding out the summer annuals. The more hardy
annuals such as calendulas may be set out even sooner,
possibly towards the end of April, and they will be in bloom
almost when the polyanthuses finish flowering early in June.

The annuals will provide valuable protection for the poly-anthuses from the hot summer sunshine where the beds are situated in open ground, whilst at the same time the polyanthus foliage will provide shelter for the less hardy annuals besides there being a great saving of expense and labour with inter-planting.

It should be remembered that annuals and all summer flowering plants to be used for inter-planting should be given soil conditions and situations similar to those in which the polyanthus are growing. Where the polyanthus is growing in a shady position, then plants used for inter-planting should also be happy in partial shade. The plants, too, should be suitable for a similar soil.

Rarely as successful as the primrose in the wild garden, the polyanthus will bloom well when planted in short grass with bulbs if in dappled and not full shade. Full shade causes the flower stems to become 'drawn' and less well able to support the large flower trusses of the modern polyanthus, whilst the colour of the bloom will be less rich than where sunshine reaches the plants. Long grass should not be cut until the end of summer when the orchard or spinney is being tidied for the winter, and so that the bloom of polyanthus and bulbs will be revealed to the full the following spring. By the end of August the polyanthus foliage will be beginning to die back whilst that of the bulbs will have already done so. The polyanthus plants will in no way be harmed if the tops of the leaves are severed for they will have served their purpose in building up a strong plant during summer to bloom in spring.

Plants growing for cut flower purposes should be planted in beds between 4 and 5 ft. wide to permit easy picking, and where cloches are to be used the plants should be set out to the exact width of the glass. Partially shaded land, which would grow little else, may be used for this purpose provided some sunshine is able to filter through to the plants. In a hundred and one ways the polyanthus may be used in the modern garden.

4

THE CULTURE OF THE POLYANTHUS IN THE HOME GARDEN

Moisture requirements—Preparation of a heavy soil—Preparation of a light soil—Planting in different soils—Obtaining the plants—Providing a mulch.

THE polyanthus will grow well in most garden soils, but if lacking in humus, as the soil of town gardens so often is, the plants will never give of their best. The difference between polyanthuses growing in soil devoid of humus and those growing in a soil well enriched with humus is more marked than is generally realised. If the plants are to be long-lived it is of the utmost importance to provide them with an abundance of moisture about the roots during summer, for should they become dry for any length of time the growth of the plants becomes stunted, and they form a woody rootstock which is detrimental to healthy plant growth. Plants growing in an open, sunny position will require a soil containing more humus than if growing in partial shade. Likewise where the plants are growing in a light, sandy soil, they will require more humus than where planted in a heavy loam. To grow good polyanthus plants it is of greater importance to provide an abundance of summer moisture than to ensure adequate drainage, for the plants will rarely be troubled by an excess of moisture about the roots as will auriculas and certain of the less vigorous double primroses, but dryness during the summer months will bring about their almost complete collapse.

It should be remembered that it is the period immediately after flowering, during the months of June and July that the plants build up their constitution for next season's flowering, no matter whether they are to be grown on for a second season without lifting, or are to be lifted and divided and replanted into freshly prepared beds to build up their vitality for flowering the following year. If because of too dry conditions, the plants are unable to make growth during this period, the display of bloom for the following spring will be

PLATE I. Polyanthus massed for spring display

Photos: Courtesy of Sutton & Sons Ltd., Reading

PLATE II. A beautiful display in a walled garden

PLATE III. Colourful Polyanthuses where little else would grow
Photos: Courtesy of Sutton & Sons Ltd., Reading
PLATE IV. Polyanthuses growing for cut flowers in a Cherry orchard

greatly reduced. The flower stems will be stunted, the individual pips will be small, whilst they will lack the richness of colour which the modern polyanthus is capable of producing. Then possibly after blooming for a single season the plants will be unable to survive another dry summer, and may die back altogether. All members of the primula family are naturally moisture-loving plants, some more so than others, and the polyanthus is no exception. For this reason it is happiest in dappled or partial shade unless it can be given a soil containing an abundance of humus. A soil unduly rich in plant food is not necessary, indeed it will cause the plants to make an abundance of leaf rather than of bloom. A limited amount of nitrogenous manure will prove of value in building up a vigorous, healthy plant with rich green foliage and a large bloom, but an excess must be guarded against.

PREPARATION OF A HEAVY SOIL

It is of interest to recall the advice given by M'Intosh in *The Flower Garden*, in which he states, 'The soil best adapted, if we may judge from the places where they grow native, must be tenacious, moist and not too rich' and he relates the methods by which one of the foremost Gold Laced polyanthus growers of the day, a Mr. Revell of Pitsmoor, Sheffield, adopted. The compost should consist of 'light maiden soil, horse-dung six weeks old, and leaf mould', the manure being used in very limited supplies, but so much depends upon the soil and upon the forms of humus to be most readily obtained. M'Intosh tells us that polyanthuses and primroses may be found growing 'in the toughest clay' which is certainly true, but clay which is shaded and moist is very different to that which is baked by the sun. Generally, then, clay soil should be enriched with humus to give the clay particles some moisture holding material during summer, whilst at the same time it will assist winter drainage.

A particularly heavy soil, often to be found when making a new garden, should first be treated with caustic (unhydrated) lime, the action of the lime as it disintegrates also breaking up the clay particles to a considerable degree. This may be applied at any time of the year except perhaps during the dry months of May and June. Then during early autumn, when the display of summer flowering plants will be at an end, the beds should be cleared and the soil enriched with humus

B

materials, depending upon those obtainable. Good quality peat is most valuable, also old mushroom bed compost. Leaf mould, provided it is true mould and not just dead leaves, used hops, and shoddy, each of which should be readily obtainable in some part of the country, will also be valuable. The material should be deeply dug in as the ground is being cleared of all perennial weeds. Where it can be obtained, some very well decayed cow or farmyard manure should be incorporated, for this, like the shoddy and the hops, will provide valuable plant food in addition to the humus.

A valuable source of humus and plant food may be made up by composting moistened straw with an activator, incorporating some dry poultry manure to encourage the straw to heat up. The heap should be turned once each week for about a month, adding additional moisture where required, when the straw will have become a rich brown colour and will be ready to use. Decayed refuse from the compost heap will have a certain value where other material is unobtainable, though it should not be sticky or it will cause more harm than good.

Especially where inter-planting is to be done and the polyanthus left undisturbed for possibly two years, it is important that the ground be thoroughly cleaned, for it will be difficult to clear the strong rooted perennial weeds when once it has been planted. Incorporate the humus at the same time, then allow the bed a week or ten days to settle down before planting.

Where the soil is heavy and the garden low-lying, it will be advisable to raise the bed several inches above the surrounding ground. This will allow excess moisture to drain away during winter, which might prove detrimental to the plant roots if heavy rains continue for any length of time. A slightly raised bed will also display the plants to their best advantage. As has been said, a bed fully exposed to the sun, and where the soil is heavy, will require considerably more humus than where it is shaded. Polyanthus plants should not be planted anywhere where there is likelihood of the soil becoming baked hard, for the plants would give only a poor account of themselves even if they were to survive for very long. Polyanthuses are tolerant of considerable moisture about their roots and a bed of heavy soil if enriched with humus and slightly raised should not require the addition of other drainage materials.

PREPARATION OF A LIGHT SOIL

A light, sandy soil, which tends to dry out in summer, will never grow such sturdy plants as a heavier loam, unless well fortified with humus materials. With a heavy soil, humus is needed to disperse the clay particles so preventing the soil from 'panning' and improving drainage, whilst with a sandy soil, humus is required for the retention of as much summer moisture as possible. Where growing polyanthus plants on a light soil in Somerset, it was necessary to incorporate as much as ten tons of humus to the acre if twice daily watering was to be reduced during May and June. Even then, vast quantities of water were needed on alternate days, and often more frequently, to keep the plants healthy during the early summer months when building up strong crowns for flowering the following season. Where in partial shade, a light soil well enriched with humus should be capable of supporting healthy plant growth even during periods of prolonged dryness. Liberal quantities of peat, used hops, shoddy, old mushroom bed compost and decayed farmyard manure should be used as liberally as possible, incorporating to a depth of at least 18 inches. Where manures cannot readily be obtained, use peat or leaf mould and give the beds a dressing with hoof and horn meal or bone meal at the rate of 2 ozs. per square yard, working this in with the humus. Apart from a dressing of sulphate of potash in early spring, to give the blooms additional richness of colour, the polyanthus requires no inorganic fertilisers which only tend to scorch the roots and produce an unnatural forcing condition which the plants will not tolerate.

Polyanthuses may be inter-planted or carpeted with violas, either the winter flowering varieties or those for summer bedding, for they appreciate exactly the same soil conditions and situation.

PLANTING IN DIFFICULT SOILS

A good quality loam will grow good polyanthuses without the additon of much humus, but sufficient should be given to help with winter drainage and to retain summer moisture. However, loams vary considerably and what constitutes a good loamy soil in a country garden, possibly where the soil is of similar type to a greasy Kettering loam and sure to grow top class blooms, would be very different to the almost inert and acid soil of a town garden though the texture might be similar. Polyanthuses will grow well in a town because of their sturdy constitution and their habit of dying back during winter when soot deposits do not choke the pores of the foliage. But this does not mean that the plants will prove happy in an old town garden where the soil will have become extremely acid and inert and be suitable only for growing privet and laurel. The plants grow best under neutral soil conditions, where the pH value is around 7.0 or very slightly acid, and where the soil is of a too acid nature, a good dressing of lime should be given two or three weeks before planting takes place. Then incorporate some decayed manure, used brewery hops or bone meal, together with some peat of good quality which will be only slightly acid. A soil, however acid and inert, thus enriched, will grow top class polyanthus blooms in the midst of an industrial city.

The polyanthus will rarely grow to perfection in a chalky soil unless well enriched with humus, for such a soil will generally be shallow and become extremely hot during summer, unless of course the plants can be given a northerly or semi-shaded position. First incorporate plenty of humus, but no lime should be given for a too alkaline soil will be as detrimental as one which is too acid. Poor grade peat, which has a high acid content, should be incorporated to correct an over-alkaline soil and also to provide humus. Decayed manure, used hops and material from the garden compost heap will all help to add depth to a shallow soil and help it to remain cooler in summer. The more time that can be taken in the preparation of the beds the better will be the reward with a healthy plant and blooms of finer quality. Also the display of bloom will be greatly prolonged, plants in a cool, moist soil remaining in bloom for fully twelve weeks.

The display may also be prolonged by selecting different situations for the beds. Plants in an open, sunny position being the first to bloom and the first to finish, whilst those growing in partial shade or in a northerly position will be later into bloom and will extend the season until well into June, very desirable where the best of the modern polyanthus strains are being grown and one can never have too much of their great beauty.

OBTAINING PLANTS

Polyanthus plants may be raised at home from seed, or they may be purchased either as seedlings or young transplanted plants from a specialist grower. The named varieties may be obtained as rooted offsets or divisions. They may be planted out at almost any time of the year with the exception of the dry months of May and June, and January and February where gardening in the North and when the ground will generally be frozen or snow covered. The most popular time for making up new beds will be in autumn, during late October when the summer bedding plants have finished flowering. Young plants will be ready for their permanent beds from a spring sowing having first been transplanted in the seedling stage to boxes or specially prepared open ground beds or frames. These young seedlings may be obtained during July and August and after a period in the beds (or boxes) will be ready for their flowering quarters in October or early November. Purchasing seedlings of the best strains is an inexpensive way of obtaining the plants where one is prepared to do, and has facilities for, transplanting. Where this is not practicable, the young plants should be obtained during autumn, depending upon when the summer display has ended. It is, however, not advisable to delay planting later than mid-November, for the plants may not become sufficiently well rooted before the arrival of hard frosts which may lift the plants from the ground and so cause injury to the roots. In the mild climate of the South-West, planting may take place at any time during winter though to have the plants in bloom the following spring, mid-November should again be the latest date for planting.

Where the seed has been sown towards the end of summer, following its harvesting in June and early July, the seedlings should occupy the frames or seed pans until the end of March when they will be transplanted to open ground beds where they remain through summer. The ideal time to make up the polyanthus beds is during October when the soil is still comfortably warm and moist and the sun will not prove troublesome. Where possible, prepare the beds at the beginning of the month and plant towards the end.

When obtaining the plants for autumn planting make sure that they have been transplanted, so that they will be sturdy and contain an abundance of fibrous roots. Plants from overcrowded seed rows or frames will never give good results. And so that the roots do not dry out in the post, ask, when sending the order, that they be sent packed in damp moss. If upon arrival it is not possible to plant immediately, open up the plants and after moistening the moss, place in a cool, shaded room then plant as soon as possible. Never at any time, from the moment the seed is sown, should polyanthuses suffer from lack of moisture, especially in the seedling or young plant stage.

Before planting, rake down the soil to a fine tilth when in a suitable condition, and whilst planting see that the roots are kept covered to protect them from drying winds. Plant the roots deeply and place the plants well into the soil so that the crown is exposed. Make them quite firm, even by treading if the soil is friable, though where of a heavy nature merely press firmly with the hand. If the soil is dry, and autumn is frequently a dry period, water in the plants thoroughly, one application generally being all that is necessary as night dews will provide the requisite moisture. The plants will require no further attention until the end of March, when they should be carefully looked over and any that have become loosened pressed back into the soil. After this has been done, take the hoe between the plants to stir up the soil which will usually have become encrusted with the weight of the winter snows and rains.

Where exhibition quality blooms are desired, lightly fork between the plants 2 ozs. per square yard of sulphate of potash where the soil is light, and half that amount where of a heavy nature, and as soon as the flower stems appear, give the plants a watering with dilute manure water once each week until in full bloom. For this, use a can without a nozzle so that the foliage will not be splashed and there will be no chance of 'burning'. After applying the manure water, spray the plants, foliage included, with clean water. Especially during dry periods will the plants appreciate a daily syringe and at all times see that the roots never lack moisture. Where growing in a shaded or northerly situation and the ground has been well prepared, little or no artificial watering should be required. Plants growing in an exposed position or in a light soil containing little humus may require additional waterings to those provided by the rain.

PROVIDING A MULCH

The plants will appreciate a mulch given when in bloom, or immediately afterwards where they are to remain in their beds, though this will be governed by spring or summer plants growing between. A mulch will help to maintain moisture in the soil whilst providing the plants with a medium into which the new roots formed from the crown of the plant at soil level, may obtain nourishment and moisture. A mulch is of the utmost importance where the plants are to be grown on for several years without disturbance and for where they are to be propagated by root division or from rooted offsets. Plants which receive no mulch will become woody and will make little new growth and so will fail to produce offsets or crowns for division. It is during June and July that the plants build themselves up for the display the following spring and a mulch will give them every encouragement.

The mulch may be of peat, decayed manure or leaf mould, and possibly to give best results it will be composed of a little of each thoroughly mixed together, the leaf mould and manure being placed through a riddle, the peat being mixed in afterwards. Equal quantities of each should be used, the mixture being worked right up to the crown of the plants with the fingers. Where possible, a 2-inch deep mulch between the plants will suppress annual weeds and will prevent a heavy soil from 'panning'. The mulch will be gradually worked into the ground thereby bringing it to a high state of fertility.

Given attention to detail in their culture, polyanthuses will make large, bushy clumps in eighteen months and will be ready for lifting and dividing after flowering for two seasons. To allow the plants to remain too long in the beds will cause the bloom to become smaller and the stems shorter. After lifting and dividing, the plants may be replanted into their original flowering quarters after the soil has been enriched with humus, or they may be replanted in specially prepared beds where they remain throughout summer, being constantly watered and provided with a mulch in July. The plants will be bedded out again in autumn. It is advisable to select a shaded piece of ground for their summer quarters.

5

THE POLYANTHUS AS A CUT FLOWER

The commercial qualities of the polyanthus—The use of cloches—
Providing moisture.

WITH its long sturdy stem and brilliance of colouring, the
modern polyanthus has become one of the most popular of
all spring flowers for cutting. No spring flower has a steadier
demand with florists, for it is the ideal flower for the small
room of the modern house and flat. It does not drop its
petals, whilst no early spring flower can equal its richness of
colouring. The bloom in its modern colour range makes a
more welcome change from the daffodil than did the older
yellow and white polyanthus blooms. The polyanthus also
enjoys a long season in bloom, from March, where grown
under cloches, until almost the end of May from shaded beds
in the open. It therefore bridges the gap between the early
daffodil arrivals in the shops and the first summer flowers
such as pyrethrums. And though the earlier bloom will
command the highest prices, even late bloom is generally
economical to produce, for the plants then require no protection and of course no heat throughout their culture. The
plants may thus be recommended to the hardy plant grower
who now finds that the cost of glasshouse heating is no longer
profitable. This is also a valuable plant to grow in the cold
northerly areas, where frosts are troublesome or where the
land is too shaded to grow other plants to satisfaction. The
polyanthus too, is a dual-purpose plant, in that it brings in
returns almost throughout the year, seedlings in summer,
young plants in autumn and in spring, divisions after flowering
and of course cut bloom during spring and early summer.
The commercial culture of the polyanthus may indeed
become a full-time business, and has a special appeal to
women gardeners who are specially fitted for transplanting
seedlings, and picking and bunching the bloom. The polyanthus is also less troubled by the weather than most plants
when in bloom, for strong winds have little effect and heavy

rains are rarely experienced during the time of year when it is in bloom in the open. The early bloom may be protected from the more adverse weather of early spring by covering with cloches.

Where the plants are being grown in Cornwall and in sheltered valleys of Devon, they will come into bloom during February quite unprotected if the winter is mild. Bloom of the best strains marketed at this time of the year will be in great demand and will make high prices, as much as 30s. a dozen bunches where the colours are rich and the stems long. Against this, of course, must be set the high rail costs when sending the bloom to Covent Garden and the large Northern markets. The plants would require no protection if growing in a sheltered position, though cloches should be on hand in case the weather became cold. Early polyanthus bloom will well repay the cost of cloches.

In the South-West, small growers plant strips of anemones, violets and polyanthuses, setting out the plants in summer and again in autumn so as to have cut bloom over as long a period as possible beginning early in the New Year. The sale of violet plants and runners in early summer will augment the sale of plants and cut bloom of the polyanthus. The plants are generally given an open, sunny situation facing south where they will receive the maximum of early summer sunshine. Dwarf hedges or turf 'walls' are used to protect the plants and blooms from strong salt laden winds, which may cause the foliage and blooms to become brown at the edges. Where there is no protection, boards may be placed round the bed to prevent wind damaging the blooms if the plants are in any way exposed.

THE USE OF CLOCHES

Where possible, by planting strips 3 ft. 6 ins. wide on various parts of the holding, in a position of full sun in the dappled shade of an orchard and in a shaded or northerly position, the flowering period will be extended by several weeks. Away from the South-West those plants required to bloom early should be covered either with barn-type cloches or with Ganwick cloches, the 'Double 18' size being 3 ft. 9 ins. wide and 18-ins. high and is ideal for covering a 3 ft. 6 ins. wide strip of polyanthus plants during March and if necessary until mid-April. Ganwicks may then be transferred to beds of strawberry plants. They may later be used to cover dwarf tomatoes or melons and the autumn-fruiting strawberries in October and November, to be placed over winter lettuce when the strawberries have finished. There they remain until required for the polyanthus plants about March 1st or early in February in the South. In this way the Ganwicks will pay for themselves in a single year, for not only will the produce be a full month earlier than that of uncovered plants, but it will be perfectly clean, free from soot and rain deposits and so will make additional returns at the markets. Cloches will also prevent the bloom of polyanthuses from being splashed with soil during heavy rains. The blooms will make quite high prices until mid-April when it has to withstand competition from outdoor-grown daffodils and lower returns should be expected from that time until the blooming ends. It is therefore important to take advantage of every sunny day of early spring by covering the plants for earliest bloom, and this will mean planting the beds in spring or early summer so that the plants are well established before winter. Some growers plant early in September and cover the plants early in November when the autumn-fruiting strawberries are coming to an end. In this way the plants are kept growing throughout the winter months and will send up their first bloom by mid-February when it will be extremely profitable. This is, however, possible only where there is a mild winter climate and an abundance of sunshine, otherwise it is better to cover towards mid-February so that the plants come into bloom in March. It may be said that plants which have enjoyed a rest period during winter, with possible freezing, will respond vigorously to cloche covering and produce finer bloom than where they are covered throughout the winter months.

Where cloches are to be used it will be necessary to plant the beds to the same width or slightly less. This will be 3 ft. 6-ins. where Ganwicks are to be used and 12-ins. for ordinary barn cloches. The 18-ins. high Ganwicks will allow more headroom which is an important consideration with the vigorous modern polyanthuses. The plants should be set out 6-ins. apart and the same distance between the rows so that seven rows may be planted beneath a double Ganwick. Where the plants are not to be covered, beds of similar width should be made up to permit the bloom to be removed without treading between the plants and causing excessive consolidation of the soil. This close planting, so necessary to utilise the glass to full advantage, may encourage mildew so it is advisable to dust the foliage regularly with flowers of sulphur until the flower buds commence to open. Throughout the winter months, watering should be done with care, applying it only to the soil between the plants so as not to splash the foliage and only when the ground begins to dry out. After planting in early autumn and until the end of October, which is generally a dry, sunny period, the plants will require copious amounts of water. Then with the approach of the dull, moist days of November, artificial watering should be withheld altogether and given only when the soil begins to dry out. This may be towards the end of February where the plants have been covered from the beginning of the month. Where the soil has been well enriched with humus in the form of the materials mentioned in the previous chapter, and the plants are to bloom unprotected, they should obtain sufficient natural moisture, though artificial watering may be necessary for the first weeks after planting and until the plants are well established. Where the soil is light and sandy, planting should be done on the flat, but where on the heavy side, beds raised about 3 inches above ground level will encourage surplus water to drain away so that the soil will warm more quickly with the rays of the spring sunshine. Vigorous plant growth in spring will not take place until the soil begins to warm, hence to enjoy early bloom it is necessary to plant in a friable, well-drained soil and preferably in a southerly situation. Everything possible should be done to encourage the plants to bloom as early as possible, for as the season advances almost every day will see a slight fall in market returns and the more bloom that can be marketed before mid-April, the more profitable will be the crop.

Plants that are to be covered during winter should be ventilated whenever conditions permit, for the polyanthus will never bloom well in a stuffy atmosphere. Except during periods of dense fog, experienced in or near the industrial towns during November, December and January, and during periods of severe frost or cold northerly winds, the plants should be allowed a free circulation of air by partially opening the ends of the cloche rows. On all sunny days when the blooms have begun to open, the cloches may be removed completely, though heavy rain should be guarded against or it may spoil the bloom.

It is not advisable to cover previously cloched plants for a second season unless the plants are lifted, divided and replanted after flowering into freshly prepared beds. Seedling plants always respond better to cloching. Where plants are to bloom unprotected, planting should be about 10 inches apart so that after giving a mulch in June, the beds may be left undisturbed to bloom a second season when the plants should be lifted and divided.

PROVIDING MOISTURE

To grow top quality polyanthus bloom, the plants should be always kept moist about the roots. Where the soil dries out, even for short periods, the flower buds may fall off without opening, whilst those blooms which do open will be small and the stems short. Where the roots are kept dry for long periods, the plants will make little growth and die back, whereas well-grown plants will make luxuriant growth during spring and summer before they begin to die back early in winter. Soil which is kept continually moist will ensure luxuriant growth and a large, richly coloured bloom on a long stem and where the plants are growing in an open, sunny position it may be necessary to water artificially between mid-March and mid-July when the plants are coming into bloom and making fresh growth. Where growing on a large scale, a hose pipe with a fine spray should be used, for the plants will appreciate a mist-like spray over their foliage. Where the soil has been well prepared, this may be sufficient to keep the plants growing and the foliage crisp and luxuriant, but where the soil tends to dry out, possibly where the plants are growing on a southerly slope and the soil is of a sandy nature, heavier applications of water may be necessary. The hose should be taken along the rows on either side of the rows of cloches where the ground is given a thorough soaking whenever the soil is dry but taking care not to splash the blooms. It is generally plants growing on the dry eastern side of Britain that will require assistance with moisture and this should be augmented by a mulch when flowering has ended. All polyanthus plants, whether growing in the home garden or commercially, will appreciate a spraying with clean water during dry periods, the early evening being the most suitable time. The plants will rarely be troubled by excessive moisture but dry conditions will be fatal, and for this reason plants

growing on the drier parts of Britain generally need some help
in spring and early summer.

CARE OF THE PLANTS

Where the plants are to be left undisturbed to flower for a
second season, when they will be at their best where grown
well and have not been allowed to suffer from lack of
moisture, they should be given a heavy mulch after flowering.
This may consist of peat, used hops, leaf mould which is well
decayed or old mushroom bed manure. A small quantity of
well-rotted farmyard or cow manure may be mixed with the
mulching material which should be placed as near to the plants
as possible. This will not only reduce watering and weeding
to a minimum, but will enable the surface roots to be protected
from the hot sun and will enable them to obtain additional
nourishment during June and July when forming strong plants
for next season's flowering. Before giving the mulch, take
the hoe through the rows though where the plants have
been set out closer together under cloches it may be necessary
to weed by hand, using a small garden fork. Here the mulch
should be placed around the plants with a trowel. Where the
plants may have made luxuriant summer growth and become
overcrowded, alternate plants, or those which appear too
crowded, should be lifted, divided and replanted into freshly
prepared beds. It is often said that after flowering for one or
two seasons the plants should be lifted and destroyed, as the
blooms will become smaller and smaller if grown on. Where
the plants have been grown well, in soil well enriched with
humus and where kept moist throughout the summer, there is
no reason at all why the plants should not be lifted and
divided indefinitely in alternate years or every year after
flowering. I have grown the American strains, which are much
too beautiful to destroy, for ten years without any deterioration
in quality of plant or bloom and after all, such fine varieties
as Barrowby Gem and Bartimeus are still vigorous after half a
century in spite of what may be said to the contrary by those
who do not grow the polyanthus well.

Plants which are to be grown on should never be allowed
to set seed, for this will greatly reduce their strength which
the plants need for next season's flowering. Plants cannot be
expected to form sturdy new growth as well as set seed and
then bear quality bloom the following spring. They will

deteriorate rapidly if allowed to set seed, so all dead blooms should be removed as soon as they are noticed, cutting away the stem as close to the crown as possible in the same way that the bloom is removed for market or for indoor decoration.

Where growing for market it may happen that a certain quantity of bloom will be spoilt by the weather or may be mis-shapen and unfit for bunching, but this should be removed and placed on the compost heap so that it does not set seed. Also, towards the end of the season, where the bloom may not prove sufficiently profitable to market, it should be removed for the same reason, the plants being looked over as soon as they have finished flowering.

It should be said that where cloches or frames are being used, the glass should always be kept quite clean by washing with soap and water. Glass which is not clean will cause both the flower stems and the foliage of the plants to become 'drawn' and weakly, whilst the blooms will lack depth of colour. For this reason, the blooms of the polyanthus are always brightest where growing in a coastal district, where the air is clearer than elsewhere. And though, like figs, the polyanthus always grows best in sight of the sea, this is only so where the generally sandy soil is well enriched with humus.

Where there is a Dutch-light greenhouse available, the polyanthus might be grown as a profitable indoor early spring crop, for the plants would occupy the house between the tomato crops. If the tomato crop was cleared by mid-October, the plants could be set out without delay, the soil following the tomato crop being of ideal quality for the polyanthus. Well-established plants should be used, preferably second year plants which have not been allowed to form bloom during the first spring in the open ground beds. By October the plants will have formed large clumps and they should be lifted with as large a ball of soil as possible. They should be planted 12 inches apart so that four rows may be planted down each side of the glasshouse. Only a Dutch-light house will prove suitable, for a low roof house with benches will neither permit sufficient light nor fresh air to reach the plants. Of all hardy plants, the polyanthus will most resent any attempt at forcing.

After planting, water well, dust with green flowers of sulphur and then water only when necessary. As much fresh air as possible should be given, opening the doors and venti-lators on all favourable occasions, closing them only at night, during foggy weather or during periods of hard frost. Otherwise the plants will require little attention until mid-February when the side glass should be shaded to protect the plants from the warm spring sunshine. Then as the plants come into bloom, admit as much air as possible and syringe them daily with clean water.

The plants may also be grown in this way under frame lights, using preferably Dutch-lights or the more usual garden light. The plants should be set out early in October, the soil first having been enriched with peat or leaf mould and some decayed manure. Second season plants should be used and given as much ventilation as possible throughout winter. The plants, both in frames or in a greenhouse will come into bloom from about March 1st and may be allowed to bloom until mid-April when the beds will be prepared for the new season's tomato crop. No form of heating should be used for the polyanthus and so it is a profitable crop for a cold house and where the tomato crop will be planted later than when heat is employed.

6

CUTTING AND MARKETING THE BLOOM

The value of polyanthus for cutting—Cutting and bunching—Packing
the bloom—Marketing the bloom—Home decoration.

WHERE growing polyanthuses for market, the blooms will
travel well if well presented, the new colours now bringing
this flower considerable popularity. Where growing for cut
bloom, a suitable shed or bunching room should be available.
If constructed of brick or stone, it will remain cool during
summer, for although the polyanthus will have finished
flowering by then, other cut flower plants such as the
pyrethrum and scabious, to be followed by dahlias and
gladioli may be grown for succession, spray chrysanthemums
and Michaelmas daisies completing almost a full twelve
months of cut flowers. With the polyanthus in spring may be
grown wallflowers, violets, primroses, and a number of bulbs
such as muscari, snowdrops and daffodils, each of which may
be naturalised so that ground not suitable for growing other
plants will be utilised. The polyanthus will fit admirably
into the cropping plans of the cut flower grower and by
growing in various aspects in the open, under cloches or
frames, a long succession of cut bloom will be available.

CUTTING AND BUNCHING

The bloom should be cut when nicely showing colour and
in the early morning, fresh with the night's dew. Always
use a pair of scissors for cutting, for the stems are strong and
to pull them carelessly will be to dislodge the plant and
sever the roots. Remove the stem as close to the crown as
possible; lengths of stems should never be left on the plant to
decay, whilst the florist will require the bloom with as long a
stem as possible. Place the blooms in a large Sussex trug
basket and remove to the packing shed without delay, for
though there is not so great an urgency at this time of the year
with the fear that a warm sun will cause the blooms to wither,
where the blooms are to travel for any distance they should

be given the greatest possible care. Look over the plants once each week during February and early March, twice each week during the latter weeks of March and three times during April and May, cutting for the most profitable market days. These will generally be Tuesday, Wednesday and Friday, the bloom being picked on the previous day, or where marketing locally, just before required.

After removing the bloom to the packing room, it should be sorted so that any dead or damaged blooms may be removed. Sometimes the edges of the petals may be brown and a single damaged pip will spoil a whole bunch. Where otherwise the truss is perfect, an odd bloom which is damaged may be removed together with its footstalk.

The bunches should contain about 8-9 stems where the trusses or heads are large and solid, or about a dozen stems where the blooms are smaller. The blue, yellow, scarlet and pink shades may be bunched separately, or mixed bunches may be made up. Where this is done, the darker colours, the smoky blue, coffee and crimson shades should be mixed with bloom of yellow, orange and corn colour, so that the bunch will not be too dark. Other attractive colour combinations are the new pinks and blues together; crimson and white; orange, yellow, tangerine and scarlet shades together. The more artistic presentation of colours will bring its reward, for the modern polyanthus and its exciting new colour range now makes it possible to present the bloom in a most attractive fashion. Just as there is a new interest in new colours and schemes for home decoration, the raisers of the modern polyanthus have been able to satisfy this new interest with a great improvement in quality.

The blooms should be arranged in tiers in the bunch so that their full beauty is revealed when in the box, from which they are generally sold by the florist. The stems should be trimmed and a rubber band inserted over the stems immediately beneath the blooms and again at the end of the stems. This will keep the bunch tidy and secure during its journey. The blooms should then be given a long drink, possibly for 2-3 hours away from the sun or any draught. A suitable method is to fill a galvanised tank with water and from a frame of wire netting over the top, the bunches are suspended with the lower part of their stems in the water. After several hours, the frame is lifted off and placed across two arms of wood or iron fixed in angle fashion to the wall above the tank, and where the water will drain from the stems before the boxes are made up. Never pack bunches with wet stems or the bloom will be damaged and the bunches may become a soggy mass if kept closed up for any length of time.

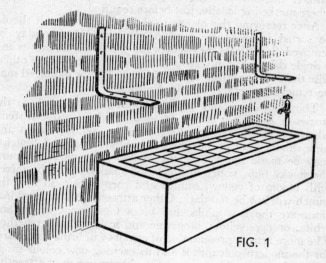

FIG. 1

PACKING THE BLOOM

Polyanthuses and all short-stemmed flowers such as anemones and violets are marketed in what are known as 'anemone' boxes. These are made of strong cardboard and are 20 inches long and 17 inches wide. Air holes and wooden reinforcements ensure the safety of the bunches and their arrival in a fresh condition. Packing the bunches calls for the greatest attention to detail. Crushing of the bloom in an attempt to get as many bunches as possible into the box will result in badly bruised flowers, whilst loosely packed bloom will be badly shaken about if it has to go any great distance. It is of little use producing a bloom of top quality if it is badly packed. First spread over the bottom of the box a sheet of white paper of good quality. Thin, poor quality paper will look the worse for its journey upon arrival at the florist's. The paper should be of a size which will enable it to be wrapped over the bloom when the boxes have been made up.

The number of bunches to a box will depend upon their size and length of stem. Bloom produced under glass where the stems will be rather longer than those of unprotected plants should be placed twelve bunches to a box in three's, two rows of three bunches at either end of the box with their stems to the centre. Small canes placed firmly across the box immediately below the blooms will hold the bunches in position and will also provide additional support for the box. Correct labelling of the box will ensure it reaching its destination safely and quickly, for everything must be done in this respect. The growing of quality polyanthus bloom is only halfway towards success, satisfactory presentation being equally important.

MARKETING THE BLOOM

The bloom must be despatched to reach the markets in time for the early morning sales and this will mean despatching in the early afternoon of the previous day. Train departures must be ascertained so that suitable connections may be made and so the boxes will be made up in time for them to arrive at their place of departure in time.

Where growing on a considerable scale it will be advisable to make up and consign boxes of 'specials' to one salesman and to send 'seconds' to a different salesman, in boxes of eighteen or twenty-four bunches, for it will prove unprofitable to send bloom of poor colouring or with somewhat short stems with that intended for top class florist's trade. Indeed, second quality bloom may well be marketed locally or used in the home. Polyanthuses present little difficulty in their bunching and arranging, for their stems carry no foliage whilst the flower heads will mostly be of similar proportions.

The bloom may either be sent to the wholesale markets to be handled by the salesman or direct to florists who are always willing buyers of quality polyanthus bloom, especially during the early weeks of spring. But before despatching any bloom, even before growing it, make contact with either salesman or florist to find out what colours are most appreciated, for requirements differ throughout the country. Birmingham and Covent Garden markets favour the pastel shades, the pale blues, coral pinks, pale yellows and buff colours, whilst the Northern markets prefer the deeper, richer colours, the reds and crimsons, tangerine and terra-cotta shades. Again, Northern markets favour a larger bunch and a bunch of mixed colours, whilst the markets of the South appreciate bunches of almost self colours, the housewife preferring to do her own mixing to suit her colour scheme at home. The most popular market days should also be discovered, though Tuesday and Friday are most popular throughout the country. And always select a wholesaler of repute, and having done so, endeavour to maintain a high standard and regular supplies. If a reputation for growing good polyanthus bloom has been built up, the local florists will seek out one's consignments and be prepared to pay top prices. In this way, grower, salesman and florist form a mutual appreciation of each other, which will prove profitable to all. An additional form of advertising will often prove profitable to the grower if his name and address is neatly printed on a small card and fastened to each bunch together with the name of the strain or variety, and the fact that the plants will be available at the appropriate time. Most poly-anthus lovers will desire to grow in their own garden a few plants of the lovely modern strains.

It really does pay to specialise whether growing anemones, violets or polyanthuses, for where space is limited supplies may then be kept up during periods of scarcity when prices will be at a peak. It may of course be possible to specialise in a number of flowers, but sufficient of one should be grown to ensure regular supplies and a full box of one or two colours though unlike violets, mixed bunches of polyanthuses may be marketed should there be insufficient of any one colour or variety to make up a full box, which frequently happens during a period of cool weather.

It is usual for the wholesaler to post details of the returns obtained from the consignment daily, immediately after the closing of the market, so that the grower will know next morning, or within forty-eight hours of forwarding the bloom, exactly where he stands. If the consignment has proved up to his expectations then it will pay him to send more whilst the market is right. If the returns are disappointing then it may pay to switch to another market or to hold the bloom if possible for several days until prices improve. The large grower will spend much of his time at the end of a telephone, just as will the dealer in stocks and shares, ruling prices being of vital importance. Indeed it is just as necessary to be a capable business man where marketing flowers as it is to be a good grower.

The colours to grow will depend upon requirements of the wholesaler or local florist, but for length of stem and rich colouring certain strains are outstanding for cutting. These include amongst English strains, Sutton's Brilliancy, Crimson King, the Broadwell strain, Toogood's Excelsior, and the Cluseed Blythe Maximum strain. Amongst the American strains, the Barnhaven Desert Sunset and Cowichan strains and the Hood River strain are excellent. The Barnhaven Blue strain and Blackmore and Langdon's Flame should also be grown, the latter for mixing in the same way that anemone growers always plant additional corms of the scarlet Hollandia to bring richness to a bunch of bloom when there may be only the more sombre colours available. For growing under cloches, the more compact strains generally used for bedding such as Carter's Sunset Hybrids, Sutton's Fancy and Blackmore and Langdon's Gold Medal strain will prove suitable, for when grown under glass the stems become longer.

HOME DECORATION

Polyanthus bloom for home decoration is at its best when used in a large bowl for table decoration. If rolled wire netting is placed in the bowl, the stems may be inserted between the wire, a liberal quantity of blooms entirely shielding the wire from view. With their sturdy stems and the brilliant colouring of the blooms the effect will be most striking, whilst the blooms will remain fresh for ten days or more if picked just as they are showing colour. Or small vases of smoked glass or earthenware jars will prove suitable, and quite delightful are the blooms when mixed with the dainty flowering miniature daffodils. Especially lovely are the Blue polyanthus and the Barnhaven Victorian strain with yellow or white daffodils.

The double polyanthuses are charming for small posy bowls and the interesting Jack-in-the-Green should not be omitted for indoor decoration. Even when the blooms are dead, the green ruff will persist for several weeks, the blooms being nipped off and other flowers being mixed with them, their ruffs providing delightful greenery for all manner of flowers, or they may be used to lend greenery to other polyanthus bloom.

A most attractive table decoration may be made by removing the bloom of the Jacks immediately behind their ruff and placing them in shallow bowls of water. They have the appearance of water-lilies and remain fresh for weeks in a cool room. For home decoration, the Jacks must be classed as amongst the most valuable of all flowers for cutting.

Whilst all polyanthus bloom carries a slight woodland fragrance, this may be made more pronounced by including a bloom of the deliciously richly almond-scented Hunter's Moon to any bunch. Its deep apricot colouring will blend with most strains. Also richly fragrant are the blooms of Carter's Orange strain, and of course Barrowby Gem. To keep the bloom as fresh and fragrant as long as possible, it should be placed in a cool room, for at no time does the polyanthus desire anything but cool conditions throughout its life. In a cool room, polyanthus bloom should remain fresh for fully a fortnight, and where a number of strains and varieties are grown, at least some bloom should be available for cutting from early March until June 1st.

7

PROPAGATION OF THE POLYANTHUS

(i) RAISING NEW VARIETIES, SAVING AND SOWING SEED

Thrum and pin-eyed flowers—Hybridising—Sowing the seed—
Preparation of the sowing compost—Care of the seedlings.

OWING to the ease with which crossing takes place, the
polyanthus is one of the most satisfying of plants to hybridise
and now that there are so many outstanding strains and
beautiful varieties, the hybridist has a considerable amount
of material to work upon. In Britain, much may be done by
crossing the best of the American and English strains in the
hope of making even further improvement.

The polyanthus, like the primrose and auricula, bears a
bloom which is either pin-eyed or thrum-eyed. In the case
of the former, the stigma which has the appearance of a pin
head, protrudes just above the end of the tube, the stamens
being inserted about halfway down the tube. With the
thrum-eyed bloom which is most common, the stigma is to be
found about halfway down the tube, whilst the stamens are
only about a quarter way down. In the one the stigma reaches
above the stamens, in the other it is below. Through insects
with long tongues, the blooms are able to pollinate each other,
but though this may easily be done it does not naturally
occur to any great extent for the plants are in bloom when
there are few long-tongued insects about. Shakespeare had
observed this, for in *The Winter's Tale* he writes,

That die unmarried, ere they can behold
Bright Phoebus in his strength . . . .

The method of crossing artificially consists of first removing
the stamens of the plant selected for seed bearing before they
begin to shed their pollen. This is necessary so that the female
flower is prevented from fertilising itself. This should be
done whilst in the bud stage, just before the bloom begins to

open. The petals are carefully removed without harming the stigma, the stamens being removed with tweezers before shedding their pollen. The exposed stigma will be pollinated by the stamens of the other selected plants whilst their pollen is still fresh. To allow the bloom to become too old, when the pollen will have become dried up will mean that it will not 'take' when applied to the stamen. The pollen will be most active when the bloom is just beginning to open and it should then be transferred to the exposed stigma with a camel hair brush.

The correct time to carry out the crossing is on a calm, sunny day preferably about mid-day when the pollen will be dry. Plants which are in any way troubled by disease should never be selected for crossing. Immediately after pollinating, the truss should be enclosed in a piece of muslin or a polythene bag tied round the stem and which should remain for three to four days. This will protect the fertilised bloom from other pollen carried by insects until the original crossing has 'taken'. The plant, together with details of the crossing, should be carefully recorded and it should be kept comfortably moist at the roots whilst setting its seed.

Whilst auriculas will not be ready for pollinating before the end of April, the polyanthus will be ready at the beginning of the month, so that it will have the generally warm, sunny days of May and June in which to ripen its seed and there should be no trouble in this respect. By the end of June, the seed should have become fully ripened and will be ready for harvesting. When this condition has been reached, the seed capsule which is divided into five segments or sections, will begin to open at the top and the stem should be removed with care and without delay, or the seed will be shed and lost. To guard against this, during June the seed pods should be inspected daily so that they may be removed at exactly the right time, just when the pods begin to open, but not before.

The full length of stem should be removed and placed on a tray over clean paper and in a dry, airy room. The seed should not be placed in the direct rays of the sun except perhaps for a few hours immediately after gathering, so that any moisture may be drained off. It is, however, better to remove the seed about mid-day and only during a period of dry weather. Should rain continue whilst the seed pods are beginning to open it will be advisable to erect a shelter over the plants. This may take the form of a 15-inch square of tin nailed to the top of a strong stake, and which when inserted into the ground will provide cover at about 2 inches above the seed head. This is more satisfactory than placing a cloche over the plant, for it will permit a free circulation of air so necessary to dry the seed.

SOWING THE SEED

A week or ten days after the seed has been removed, it should be carefully shaken from the pods which are split open so that every seed may be saved. The seed may then be sown during July or at any time up to mid-September depending upon available conditions. Polyanthus seed is small, round and of a bright deep brown colour and is very easily managed. Sowing is best done with finger and thumb, a pinch at a time. Seed that is not required to be sown until early spring should be placed in small boxes, a cedar cigar box is ideal, carefully labelled and stored in a cool, dry room. Dampness should be excluded at all costs, whilst the seed should not be stored in a too warm cupboard, one near a fire or central heating.

Specialist growers will make up packets of seed when required, and in this way a profitable side-line may be built up where the seed is saved from the best strains. The modern polyanthus strains are so outstanding that it does not pay to grow anything but the best. Over the years, certain growers have specialised in certain strains or varieties. Miss Jekyll worked to improve a yellow and white polyanthus; E. M. Wilson devoted his life to the raising of and improving the blue polyanthus, likewise Miss Linda Eickmann and the now famous Crown Pink strain. It may, however, take more than a quarter of a century for one's endeavours to attain perfection and considerable patience will be necessary to achieve the final goal.

The polyanthus is propagated either by

(a) Sowing seed, or by
(b) Root division or offsets.

Both are equally valuable methods of increasing stock but with the ease in germinating the seed, this is perhaps the most popular method of propagation and is certainly the least expensive way of obtaining a stock. Polyanthus seed is generally more reliable as to germination than the seed of its parents, the cowslip and primrose, and so may be sown entirely without heat to aid germination. Again, no plant is more flexible in its sowing times, for the seed of the polyanthus may be sown at almost any time of the year with equally satisfactory results. In this respect much will depend upon available sowing facilities. The larger grower will utilise either a frame or a cold greenhouse for sowing the seed, whilst the amateur gardener will sow in either a box or pan covered with a sheet of glass and placed in a sunny position.

A satisfactory frame may be made by the use of old railway sleepers, over which garden lights are placed. Or 8-inch boards may be held in position by stout stakes. The use of wood will prove more satisfactory than where bricks are used, for unless they can be cemented, bricks will tend to harbour slugs which will attack the young seedlings. No great depth will be required with a frame used for polyanthus seedlings, for they are of sturdy habit and will rarely grow more than 3 inches high before being transplanted.

The seed may be germinated in boxes or pans in a cold greenhouse, either on a bench or on the floor of a Dutch light house. The maximum amount of light is necessary to raise a sturdy seedling and where the greenhouse has sides of wood or brick, it will be important to sow as near to the glass as possible.

Seed may also be sown in drills in the open ground but polyanthus seed is expensive and is extremely small, and this method cannot be advised except in the most favourable areas of the South-West. Here, natural warmth combined with moisture enables rapid germination to take place if the seed is sown in June or July. It is, however, better to give the seed some degree of control where moisture, ventilation and freedom from pest attack will enable almost 100% germination to take place.

An excellent structure may be made by fixing polythene sheeting to a frame of stout timber made 6-7 ft. high and about the same dimensions in length and breadth. To give additional protection from heavy snow and rains, it will be advisable to make an apex roof of ordinary glass and sash bars which may be obtained cut to standard size. As a means of entry, an old door from a disused property will prove satisfactory and so the whole structure will cost less than

£20. Benches may be fixed to the timber frame inside the house and upon these the boxes or pans of seed are placed.

Where growing on a large scale, a sowing may be made in such a structure, or in any ordinary cold greenhouse, in a frame, or under cloches or Ganwicks, the seed being sown in early spring and again in early August thus utilising the glass to the full. Sowing twice each year also enables the seedlings to be transplanted over a longer period than where one large sowing is made. Thus the seedlings will not remain in their seed boxes, where these are used, longer than necessary when they may either damp off or become too 'drawn'.

The seed may be sown almost the whole year round. Some make a sowing in January, not in heat as might be expected, but the pans, which are covered with glass, are allowed to remain in the open. In this way the seed becomes frozen and germination will be hastened when once the weather becomes warm. Seed may also be sown in early spring, towards the end of March or early April, for by then the sun's rays are increasing in strength and germination will have taken place by the end of April. The seedlings may then be transplanted during the generally wet month of July when a second sowing may be made. This will allow the seed time to germinate and form strong seedlings to withstand the winter, when they are transplanted to open ground beds during the latter days of March and during April. No form of heat is necessary or advisable for any sowings.

A late July or early August sowing is recommended by some, for this is the time of natural sowings, soon after the seed has fully ripened and it is believed that germination will prove more complete and the seedlings will be more vigorous if a sowing is made at this time. Though it may be said that the fresher the seed the more quickly it will germinate, seed which is anything up to two years old will germinate satisfactorily and give almost 100% germination. But sowing at this time will mean that the plants will not be large enough to plant out, except perhaps in the South-West, until the following spring, and so must be wintered under cover. They will therefore not bloom until the following year, eighteen months after sowing, when they will have formed large plants and will give an abundance of bloom. They may, however, be made to bloom several months earlier by covering plants with cloches or frames, when they will come into bloom from the early New Year depending upon district and prevailing conditions. Where growing under glass this is the best time to sow, for from a spring sowing the plants would not have made sufficient growth to cover with glass.

Plants from an early spring sowing or from an early New Year sowing in gentle heat will, however, bloom the following spring, little more than twelve months after sowing, but a sowing should be made before the end of April so that the young plants have time to make plenty of growth before the autumn.

Cropping programmes must play a part in the sowing times. Spring is generally a busy time on most nurseries and holdings, and July a slack period, so that an early spring sowing may be favoured by many growers for this reason alone. This may be partially overcome in favourable areas and where the soil is light and well drained, by planting out early autumn sown seedlings at the beginning of March. This is the method followed by Messrs. Blackmore and Langdon. M'Intosh tells us that one of the most famous growers of the early nineteenth century, Mr. Revell of Sheffield, always sowed his seed in early February. The soil in the frames would sometimes become completely frozen, but with the warmer conditions of March, germination would have taken place by early April, the seedlings being transplanted early in June. This is, however, most often a dry month with the consequent difficulty in providing the seedlings with sufficient moisture and though they would have a full summer in which to make growth, my own opinion is that early spring is the best time to sow, the seedlings being transplanted early in July. They will then bloom the following spring and again the next year without the need for lifting and dividing. For those amateur gardeners wishing to raise their own plants, this would be the most suitable time, for the plants would be strong enough to survive the severest winter and would bloom less than twelve months from sowing time. But seed may be sown at almost any time of the year and this will generally be dictated by available sowing methods and the most accommodating time to transplant the seedlings.

It should be said that wherever the seed is to be sown, complete cleanliness should prevail. Boxes and seed pans should have been previously washed with SterIzal, whilst the glass of cloches, frame or greenhouse should have been washed clean with soap and water. This should be done just before the seed is sown and in industrial areas it may be necessary to do this two or three times a year, for it is vital that the maximum amount of light reaches the seedlings.

PREPARATION OF THE SOWING COMPOST

The seed may be sown either in boxes or pans, or directly into the ground beds of a Dutch light house, in a frame, or under cloches. Where sowing in prepared ground beds, the seed is generally sown broadcast. If sown reasonably thinly, the young plants may be allowed to remain until they form very much larger plants than where seed is sown in boxes and where the root run and food value is much more limited. The plants growing in boxes or pans will also require considerably more attention with their watering than those sown in ground beds. But whichever method is employed, the seed should always be sown in sterilised soil so that during the month or five weeks required for germination there will be no competition from weeds.

Where sowing in the ground, soil to a depth of 4 inches should be removed, over which the frame or cloches are to be placed. A position should be chosen which is well drained, taking care to ensure that water does not drain beneath the seedlings during winter. The seed sowing compost, whether the seed is to be sown in the open ground or in boxes or pans, should consist of a friable, sterilised loam, preferably Kettering loam which is more retentive of moisture than most soils. But if this is not readily obtainable procure a quantity, depending upon how much seed is to be sown, of good virgin pasture loam. If impossible to sterilise, or to obtain a sterilised sowing compost already prepared, obtain pasture loam from a depth of 12-18 inches, for at such a depth most weed seeds and fungus spores will be eliminated. Never use the almost inert and acid soil of a town garden, for though the seeds may readily germinate, the seedlings will never get away to a good start, and after making early growth may begin to go back or damp off before they are large enough to transplant.

To 4 parts of loam should be added 1 part coarse sand, and 1 part either peat or leaf mould and to a barrowful of the mixture should be added 2 ozs. of superphosphate to

encourage vigorous root action. This should be mixed well
in. Polyanthuses grow best in a soil which is only slightly
on the acid side, and should the mixture have a pH value less
than 6.5, lime should be added to correct excess acidity.
It is better to mix the sowing compost just previous to it
being used and to keep it under an open shed or away from
heavy rain so that when required it will be in a friable condition, just right for sowing. A very small quantity of well-
decayed cow manure or bone meal, a quarter of a pound of
the latter to a large barrowful of compost, may also be added
where the seed is to be sown in the ground and may occupy
the same place for a longer period than where sown in boxes.
For those who are to sow only a small quantity of seed, the
John Innes Sowing Compost made up to the correct formula
and obtainable from most nurserymen or seed stores will
prove satisfactory. This is composed of

> 2 parts sterilised loam
> 1 part coarse sand
> 1 part peat

to which is added $1\frac{1}{2}$ ozs. superphosphate of lime and $\frac{3}{4}$ oz.
ground limestone or chalk per bushel. This compost will
prove excellent for sowing in boxes and pans.

Another method of preparing the soil when the seeds
are to be sown in the open ground, is to first treat it
with a diluted solution of SterIzal about three weeks before
sowing. After thoroughly soaking the soil it should be turned
about for a fortnight to dry out and for the fumes to escape,
when it may be prepared for sowing by incorporating the
sand and peat and superphosphate as previously described.
After raking down to a fine tilth, the seed may be sown.

Maddock, the well-known auricula and polyanthus grower
of the early nineteenth century, said that seed should be sown
tolerably thick, being covered very lightly or not at all,
leaving the rain to wash it in. But to sow too thickly will mean
that the seedlings will become overcrowded before they can
be moved. The result will be that many may damp off,
especially where an autumn sowing has been made. For
this reason too thick sowing should be guarded against, and
where sowing broadcast in a frame, or on the ground of a
Dutch light house it is better to divide up the area into

sections so that sowing will be done evenly, an ounce of seed being sufficient for an area of about 25 square feet. The seedlings will thus have plenty of room in which to make their early growth.

Where sowing in boxes or pans, first make sure that they are well crocked to ensure efficient drainage, then place in the compost to a depth of at least 2 inches. Make quite level and reasonably firm by giving the compost a light pressing with a wooden block. Then sow the seed thinly with finger and thumb evenly over the surface. The older growers advised covering the seed with compost to a depth of $\frac{1}{4}$-inch, but this seems rather too thick a covering, $\frac{1}{8}$-inch being sufficient. It is important to cover the seed evenly otherwise germination may be irregular.

CARE OF THE SEEDLINGS

After the seed has been sown, give a thorough soaking with a fine rose and cover with brown paper to hasten germination. Seed sown in boxes or pans will also germinate more rapidly if covered with a sheet of clean glass, for this will maintain humidity and assist the hard seed to germinate. At no time should the compost be allowed to become dry, for this would greatly retard germination, whilst if the soil should at any time dry out when once germination has taken place, the tiny seedlings may suffer irreparable damage. This, however, does not mean that the compost should be kept in a soaking condition, and when to water will depend entirely on the weather. Seed sown in late summer and early autumn may require watering almost daily until mid-October, when the arrival of fogs and rain will create a more humid atmosphere. From then onwards the seedlings will require only an occasional watering until the sun begins to gather strength again early in spring.

Where the seed has been covered with paper to assist with germination, this should be removed the moment germination has taken place or the seedlings will become 'drawn' and never recover. After sowing, the compost should be inspected daily for water requirements and for germination, and where a sheet of glass has been placed over the seeds, or where sown under a frame light or cloche, it is important to keep the glass perfectly clean. Glass placed over a box or pan should be removed as soon as the seed has germinated.

From then onwards a buoyant atmosphere should be maintained, ventilating whenever conditions allow, removing the frames or cloches entirely during daytime. Where the seedlings are being grown in a greenhouse, the boxes or pans should be lifted outside whenever the weather is fair. Where the seed has been sown in early spring and germination will have taken place by mid-April, the seedlings will thoroughly enjoy being exposed to the sunshine and showers for several hours each day, or they may be placed permanently in the open from then onwards and where they will remain until ready for transplanting. Seedlings from an autumn or late summer sowing are best kept covered, though well ventilated, during the winter months, but should in no way be coddled or they will not be fit to plant out during March and will have to wait for the arrival of warmer conditions.

PLATE V.
The Polyanthus in the
woodland glade

*Photos: Courtesy of
Sutton & Sons Ltd., Reading*

PLATE VI.
Polyanthuses in the sunken
garden for spring bedding

8

PROPAGATION OF THE POLYANTHUS

(ii) PLANTING OUT SEEDLINGS AND DIVIDING PLANTS

Preparation of the ground—Transplanting the seedlings—When to lift and divide the roots—Dividing the plants—Root cuttings.

THE seedlings should be planted out when large enough to handle and when soil and climatic conditions permit. From an early spring sowing, the seedlings should have formed two or three leaves by early July which is generally a dull, rainy month and ideal for transplanting. From a late summer sowing, early spring will generally provide similar conditions when the seedlings should be transplanted without undue delay. This will allow them more room to develop and a fresh supply of plant food. For this reason, the plants should never be kept in the boxes or pans for a moment longer than necessary.

The seedlings should be planted out into specially prepared beds and a partially shaded situation should be chosen, one of dappled shade or facing north. The ground should be cleaned of all perennial weeds and should have been dug over during winter so that the frosts will break down the soil to a fine tilth. Some humus and plant food should be incorporated, for the plants will require nitrogen and potash in addition to humus to retain summer moisture. Select a position where winter rains will drain away and incorporate into the soil some peat, leaf mould, decayed cow or farmyard manure, used hops or old mushroom bed compost. Some form of organic manure should be used so as to provide the plants with the nitrogen, so necessary to make healthy growth. To provide potash to enable the plants to withstand adverse winter conditions, work in a liberal amount of wood ash which has been stored dry, or give a dressing of 2 ozs. per square yard of sulphate of potash just prior to planting. The ground should receive a light dressing with hydrated lime if the soil is at all acid and this should be given whilst the ground is being cleaned and dug over. The soil should be raked into a fine tilth before transplanting begins.

TRANSPLANTING THE SEEDLINGS

The professional method of planting out the seedlings will be to place a 9-inch board on the soil at one end of the bed on which one kneels to carry out the transplanting. The board will consolidate the ground and maintain a level surface without treading too much and causing indentations. The edge of the board will also act as a 'line', two rows of seedlings being planted out 4 inches apart each way, the board then being moved again to a similar distance. The finished bed will look completely professional and will be level and firm, whilst the seedlings will be evenly spaced throughout. Should the position be unduly exposed, 9-inch boards should be fixed along the side of the bed against the prevailing wind and held in place by stout pegs. Strong wind will cause the soil to dry out too quickly and it may be necessary to give protection until the seedlings become sufficiently well rooted. They should be well watered in after planting each strip, but it will be better if a showery period and a moist soil is experienced before any planting commences. For this reason early April and July should be chosen as the most suitable planting months, but never plant when the ground is sticky following heavy rains. The soil should be moist and friable so that it does not stick to the fingers when the seedlings are set out.

Planting should be done either with a pointed trowel or with a blunt, smooth ended stick, the seedlings being inserted well into the ground and pressed comfortably in. If the soil is sticky it will come away from the roots when pressed.

After planting, the seedlings should be kept moist so that they will grow away without check, and should the weather be unduly warm and sunny, either branches of evergreens should be placed over the bed, or wattle hurdles, or lengths of canvas should be erected on the sunny side to help to maintain cool, moist soil conditions so essential to growing good polyanthuses. During periods of drought, the young plants should be regularly sprayed each evening throughout summer.

Where the plants are to be grown on to bloom without being moved again, the seedlings should be planted 8 inches apart; or alternate plants and rows may be lifted when the plants have made full growth and may either be sold or replanted into other beds. If the plants are to be covered with cloches or Ganwicks, the seedlings should be set out to the required distance so that they will not need moving again unless a more sunny position is required. As the plants make growth, the beds must be kept clear of weeds by hand, and moist peat should be scattered over the bed as frequently as possible to help maintain moisture and give the young plants the conditions they desire.

Where ground is limited or where growing on a small scale, the seedlings may be transplanted to boxes, preferably using a box 4 inches deep so that the plants may enjoy a cool, deep root run. By growing on in boxes until ready for planting out into their permanent quarters after three or four months, the plants may be given greater supervision as to watering, protection from pest, particularly slug attack, and keeping them clear of weeds. The compost may be sterilised to eliminate pests, weed seeds and fungus spores, but it should be said that plants growing in boxes will become over-crowded more quickly as they are set out only 2 inches apart, whilst they will be restricted as to their root run. This means that they will use up the food in the compost more rapidly than where planted in the open ground, whilst they will require considerably more attention as to watering. Close planting is permitted as the plants will later be moved to their flowering beds and so will occupy the boxes for only a few months. In this way more plants may be grown on in considerably less space, the boxes being placed in a frame or in a shaded position outdoors.

Propagation by means of offsets or root division is the only means by which a named variety or one possessing certain admired qualities may be increased. Provided the plants are grown well and are not allowed to become 'woody' by growing them in a soil which has become too dry, or by failing to divide the roots at least in alternate years, there is no reason why root division should not maintain the quality of bloom to be expected from seedling plants.

WHEN TO LIFT AND DIVIDE THE ROOTS

The correct time to lift and split up the roots has long remained a debating point with gardeners and even with specialist growers, and whilst it is now most frequently recommended that plant division should take place immediately after flowering, this must be governed by soil, climate and situation. The polyanthus will continue to grow and build up a strong plant to bloom the following spring, from March until the end of August when it begins to die back, and from that time until early spring enjoys a period of dormancy. Whilst the plant will be continually forming fresh crowns or offsets around the parent plant, they will become more vigorous and form a more active root system if they are detached from the older plant. Planted on their own will give them room in which to reach maturity and remain healthy. Failure to divide frequently will cause the centre portions of the plant to lose vigour, its roots being unable to obtain sufficient food and moisture to maintain freedom and quality of blooming. Constant division is therefore important to maintain the vigour of the stock besides being an inexpensive method of increasing the stock.

Exactly when to divide will, however, be governed by soil and climate, for to divide immediately after blooming will mean that this is to take place during the dry months of May and June, and however well the ground has been prepared this is never a suitable time to establish new plantings either of offsets, root divisions or seedlings. It will be better to delay dividing the plants until early July, for this is almost always a damp, humid month. If the work is done at the beginning of the month, the plants will quickly re-establish themselves and have about ten weeks in which to make new growth before the plants enter a period of rest. Where the soil is light and well drained, the plants may be divided almost until the year end, though if required for blooming under glass, the plants should be divided during July so that they will become thoroughly established before being covered in the early New Year.

Those plants which are to be grown for cut flower purposes should be replanted in prepared ground where they are to bloom, but where required for spring bedding, the plants should be split up and planted in a shady part of the garden where they will remain until October. It may be that the plants will have occupied a bed for two seasons and are ready for dividing. This should be done towards the end of May so that the beds may be planted with the summer flowering plants. In this case it will be better to replant into partially shaded ground enriched with plenty of humus. If kept well watered, the plants should be able to withstand the usually dry period. If the flowering beds are in dappled shade, the plants may be divided and replanted where they are to bloom and they may be inter-planted with summer flowering plants. But wherever possible lift and divide during the last six months of the year, July being the most suitable time, and leave the plants undisturbed during the first six months. Liberties, however, may be taken where the plants are growing down the moister Western side of Britain, where the winter climate is less severe than on the Eastern side and a damp, humid atmosphere persists almost the whole year round. And particularly in the mild, damp climate of the South-West, dividing may be done at almost any time, though for a satisfactory display either in the open or under glass, July will be the best month for the work as elsewhere.

DIVIDING THE PLANTS

Polyanthus plants should be lifted with care so that the fibrous roots, especially those almost at the surface, will be in no way damaged. Carefully shake away all surplus soil then, firmly holding the plant, pull apart the various crowns. In the very apt words of that great gardener Miss Frances Perry, 'tease' the crowns apart. In this way each crown will come away containing its full quota of fibrous roots, whilst there will be no open wounds as may be the case where the plants are cut into sections. M'Intosh has also written that 'by cutting away the slips (offsets) with a knife, there is a tendency to destroy the root' and those who have ever used a knife for root division will recall that the offsets may have come apart cleanly but entirely without any roots. Just 'tease' them apart with care, for every crown, however small, will grow into a flowering plant. Where the plants have formed large clumps which they will do if given good cultivation, they should be divided like any other herbaceous plant, by placing two border forks back to back at the centre of the plant and gently prise apart. The two sections may then be divided as described into numerous offsets and these should be removed to a cool, shaded place without delay and where they remain until ready for replanting as soon as possible. Any unduly large leaves may be screwed off about 3 inches above the crown before replanting in the same way as when lifting and removing the tops of beetroot, for it is not necessary for the plants to have to re-establish these coarse outer leaves. Offsets with new and smaller leaves should be replanted without the removal of any foliage, for those young leaves will catch the dew and rains and direct the moisture to the roots thus enabling the plants to become more quickly established. The offsets should be set well into the ground and pressed firmly with the hand, or with the foot where the soil is friable. They should be kept well watered until established.

Small pieces, provided they contain a root, however small, may be grown on but are best planted in beds to themselves, where they may be given that little extra care until forming new roots. As much foliage as possible should be removed so that the plant will not have to support excess foliage whilst endeavouring to form new roots. So that it is given as much help as possible, a shaded position should be selected and one sheltered from strong winds which would dry out the sparse roots and cause the plant to die back before becoming established.

Though all members of the primrose family may be lifted and divided when in bud or full bloom, this is not advisable, for some bloom will be damaged and those polyanthuses with long stems will become more quickly established when the stems are removed. It is thus better to wait until July when the plants will have finished flowering.

ROOT CUTTINGS

This is another form of propagation and though not often followed, owing to the ease by which the plants may be raised from seed or offsets, it does provide a method by which rare named varieties, or those bearing bloom of unusual colouring, may be increased more rapidly than by division of the roots. Certain varieties too, are less vigorous than others in forming offsets.

The polyanthus, like the primrose, *Primula denticulata* and many other members of the family forms numerous thick, fleshy roots apart from the more fibrous surface roots. When the plant is lifted, several of these fleshy roots may be removed before the plant is divided and without being in any way detrimental. They should be removed with a sharp knife at the point where they join the crown and they should be placed in a box with the cut end in a certain position so that it may readily be identified. The roots may be 6 inches long or more and they should be cut into portions about $1\frac{1}{2}$ inches in length, always keeping the severed ends in the same direction.

After the roots of a certain variety have been cut they should be inserted singly into $2\frac{1}{2}$-inch pots containing a sandy compost, to which a little moist peat has been added to maintain moisture. The cut or severed part of the cutting should be inserted to the top in an upright position, and it should be just below the level of the compost, a little pure sand being placed over it to exclude the air and prevent it drying out. The pots should be well watered in and a sheet of glass placed over the top of a dozen or more pots to create humidity. If always kept moist, fresh green growth will soon be seen appearing from the top of the root, when the glass should be removed and the plants grown on to be planted out at a later date.

Another method is to place the root cuttings in a horizontal position over a layer of sandy compost in a seed pan. The cuttings should be just covered with compost and a sheet of glass placed over the top. Provided they are kept comfortably moist, the cuttings will soon commence to form growth when they should be removed to individual pots containing a friable compost. The more rare double polyanthuses, the hose-in-hose and rare single varieties such as Barrowby Gem, may be propagated in this way.

9

EXHIBITING THE POLYANTHUS

The Gold Laced polyanthus—Growing for exhibition—Preparing the plants for exhibition—Merits of the Gold Laced polyanthus—Merits of the ordinary polyanthus.

THROUGHOUT the early part of the nineteenth century the Gold Laced polyanthus was equally as popular as a florist's flower and an exhibition flower as the Show auricula. It was grown in pots in a similar way and was almost the only type of polyanthus then grown. The rules upon which the Gold Laced polyanthus was judged 100 years ago remain until this day only very slightly altered. It was in 1878, five years after the first show was organised by the then National Auricula Society, that a Class was introduced for the Gold Laced polyanthus, chiefly on the instigation of that grand old enthusiast Sam Barlow of Castleton. Its popularity on the show bench, however, was but short lived, for immediately after Barlow's death, the Class was discontinued and for at least a decade the Gold Laced polyanthus was excluded from future shows, though for 100 years it had been exhibited locally and always created great interest. There were Classes both for red and black ground varieties and it was not until after the First World War that prominence was given to the ordinary garden polyanthus, from which time its popularity as an exhibition flower has progressed in proportion to its popularity as a garden plant. Indeed the ordinary polyanthus has taken the place of the old Gold Laced type which was almost always grown in pots as it was not considered a suitable flower for garden decoration. The blooms do have a tendency to fade slightly where exposed to full sunlight and yet have too dark a ground colour for them to be widely used for garden decoration in full shade. For this reason they have remained an exhibitor's flower and the garden is all too often deprived of their great charm. Even a few plants set out together in a shrubbery, border or rockery, will provide considerable interest over a long period, and a position of dappled shade will suit them best. Such a situation will also be more satisfactory where growing the ordinary polyanthus strains for exhibition, for here the blooms will be shielded from the full rays of the sun, yet a certain amount of sunshine they must have to bring out the intense colouring of the blooms.

GROWING FOR EXHIBITION

Though the old growers of the Gold Laced varieties grew their plants throughout their life in pots, or at least from early autumn until the plants had flowered, it is not advisable to follow their example unless ground room is extremely restricted. The most satisfactory method is to grow plants intended for exhibition in a sheltered border until the early spring when they awaken from their winter rest and come into new growth. They are then placed into either 60 or 48 size pots which are inserted in the ground, or in beds of moist peat, until the flower buds begin to open. They should then be placed in frames or in a greenhouse-like structure, where they are kept in a buoyant atmosphere whilst the blooms are opening and until ready for the show bench.

For exhibition, second season plants should be used, those from a sowing made during July or August eighteen months previously, and which have been de-bloomed their first year, all flower stems being removed as they appear. The plants should be given a soil well provided with humus and some plant food in the form of decayed farmyard manure, or hoof and horn meal, which has been well worked in just before planting. The plants should be allowed a full square foot in which to develop and throughout spring and summer should be kept well watered, a mulch being given in early June.

The ground should be kept free of weeds and any flower stems which may appear in autumn should be removed and the ground dressed with 2 ozs. per square yard of sulphate of potash. This will give depth of colour to the blooms in spring. Then early in March, as the fresh growth appears, the plants should be lifted without disturbing the roots more than necessary. They should be planted in 48 size pots containing a compost of 2 parts loam, 1 part sand and 1 part peat or leaf mould. This should be comfortably packed round the roots, the pot first having been crocked to help with drainage.

M'Intosh suggests a compost consisting of 'I part well rotted cow dung, peat or leaf mould, I part of fine white sand, and 2 parts of hazel-coloured pasture loam, the whole being thoroughly mixed and sweetened by exposure before being used'. He also suggests that the pots be kept in a northerly or shaded place, or of course they may be kept under some form of glass covering.

To encourage the plants to build up supplies of food, they should be watered with dilute liquid manure once each week throughout summer, and this may be repeated during March and April when in the pots and until the blooms begin to show colour. Systematic feeding will build up a vigorous plant and one bearing a thick, sturdy stem and a large refined bloom of rich colour.

Another method of growing for exhibition is to sow seed under glass early in spring and to grow on the plants in the open ground until mid-November when they are lifted and potted into 60 size pots and wintered in a frame. Or rooted offsets may be removed immediately after flowering and grown on in prepared beds until early March when they are lifted and potted. They may also be grown on for another year, being fed and de-bloomed exactly as for seedling plants, when they may be exhibited the following year. Where the plants are to occupy the ground for eighteen months, the soil should be well-enriched with humus and plant food. The exact time to pot will chiefly depend upon soil texture. If the soil is light and well drained the plants may remain in the open until early March but if of a heavy, clay nature, the plants will be best lifted and potted early in November. Excess winter moisture about the plants will only cause the roots to die back and in consequence the plants will suffer when they come into bloom.

It may be advisable to lightly disbud the flower trusses so that the blooms will not be overcrowded and so will be able to open to perfection. Some disbudding will also encourage the individual blooms to attain their maximum size. The centre bud should be removed, for this will generally be smaller than the others and may upset the balance of the truss. M'Intosh has told that Revell never allowed more than seven pips nor less than five to remain on a stem, and if any pips were slightly cup-shaped he would flatten them with an ivory 'flattener' as used for auricula bloom. Pips of the

Gold Laced varieties were dusted with a camel-hair brush to give a lustre to the dark ground blooms.

The Gold Laced varieties will respond better to this treatment than will the modern large-flowered strains, but it is agreed that all polyanthus bloom required for exhibition should be sheltered from rain and the sun's rays as soon as the bloom is showing colour. Plants growing in pots in a frame or greenhouse should be sheltered from the sun by whitening the inside of the glass, or by fastening brown paper inside the glass on the southerly side. Another method is to insert the pots in rows in the ground so that they are almost touching each other and to cover with the whitened cloches. By this method the pots will obtain moisture from the ground and so will not require so much attention as to watering, which plants in pots generally require. The compost should never be allowed to become too dry, whilst the foliage will benefit from a daily syringing with clear water not only to maintain freshness but to guard against red spider.

PREPARING THE PLANTS FOR EXHIBITION

To have the bloom at its best on the day of the show calls for experience and a high degree of timing. In some seasons it may be too advanced, in others it may be too retarded and both demand experience in their correcting. A more humid atmosphere will help to bring on the bloom and shading may be reduced, but it should be remembered that the polyanthus will resent undue forcing which will only result in long, weakly stalks and a bloom which will lack colour. To retard the bloom which may be opening too soon and which may then have lost some of its quality by show day, a more buoyant atmosphere and more shading should be provided, but here again to shade too much so that the plants are deprived of ordinary light, quite apart from sunlight, will only result in a pale coloured bloom and 'drawn' stems. Much will depend upon the weather and from the beginning of April the plants should be observed with care, bringing them on or retarding them as the weather dictates. Too much rain reaching the blooms or excessive sunshine will certainly prevent the Gold Laced varieties from being exhibited at their best, but the ordinary polyanthuses are much more able to combat adverse conditions, hence their greater popularity with the modern gardener.

Where taking the plants to the exhibition, and the Gold Laced polyanthus is always exhibited in its pot, which should be quite clean, it is advisable to fasten the flower stems to a small wooden stick to prevent the truss from breaking. It should be remembered that the stems, though strong, will have to support a heavy weight, with possibly a dozen or more blooms open together. The stem should be made secure immediately beneath the truss and again lower down the stem, using wide raffia so as not to cut through the stem should the plant on its journey be subjected to any shaking. The plants should be placed four to a wooden box and they should be shaded from strong sunlight. Should any pips (blooms) have become damaged, possibly at the edges, they should be removed together with the footstalk and though this may upset the balance of the truss it is better than to have it spoilt by a single damaged pip.

In most shows, there is provided a Class for cut polyanthus bloom of the ordinary strains, and this will allow the enthusiast considerable liberty in the selection and arrangement. Here, not only quality but selection of colours plays its part and with the modern strains, especially those from America, some outstanding new colours may be introduced, though of course quality must be given first consideration.

In taking the cut bloom to the show, if a dozen blooms are required to be exhibited, then at least twenty should be taken so that the best may be selected on the show bench, and this will allow for any damage to stem or bloom on the journey. The blooms should be fully open, but only just so, for they will then travel well and will be exhibited at their best. Cut the bloom with as long a stem as possible early on the day of the show and place the stems in cold water. After giving a drink for as long as possible, carefully dry the stems before packing into either a wooden or cardboard flower box. Each stem should be placed separately in the box, rolls of good quality tissue paper being placed beneath each flower head to lend support. The stems should also rest on paper rolls to prevent them breaking. They are held in position by placing thin canes across the box. When exhibiting in pots, each variety, strain or seedling which is an unnamed poly-anthus and which has been raised from seed by the exhibitor, should be clearly named on the small cards supplied by the show societies. The Gold Laced polyanthus is classed with the

Show and Alpine auriculas in that a plant should bear a minimum of five expanded blooms, and this will be confined to a single main stem. No packing is allowed between the footstalks so as to help in the correct placement of the blooms, but these may be used in conveying the plants to the show.

MERITS OF THE GOLD LACED POLYANTHUS

The merits of a good Gold Laced polyanthus were laid down by the old florists of more than a century ago and have been changed but little. The foliage should be fresh, clean and healthy. The stem should be about 6 inches in length, the peduncles or footstalks being of such a length to bring the pips together in perfect symmetry. The truss should have not less than six opened blooms. Some little time ago the minimum was five blooms and during the hey-day of the Gold Laced auricula, as few as three blooms were allowed, but this did not take into consideration the symmetry of the truss in the desire to obtain near perfect blooms and so the natural form of the polyanthus bloom was given little or no consideration.

Samuel Barlow, that great enthusiast of the Gold Laced polyanthus during the mid-nineteenth century, advocated that the blooms should be between $\frac{3}{4}$ and $\frac{7}{8}$ inches in diameter. The bloom should be flat, perfectly circular and smooth; the petals should be without serrations. Each bloom will be composed of five or six petals, the gold edging or lacing being continued down the inside segments or petals and round the outside, though the slight overlapping obscures the lacing down the insides.

The blooms should be thrum-eyed, a pin-eye disqualifying the plant. The anthers should curl slightly inwards and cover the stigma in the tube which should be quite round and at the centre of the bloom. It is important that the lacing be thin, of regular width, and unbroken, whilst the body or ground colour should not in any way 'run' into either the lacing or the centre or eye, which should be perfectly circular and of a clear golden colour. The ground or body colour should be either black or crimson-red. Sam Barlow called it Indian Red and which should have a velvet-like texture. In the perfect Gold Laced bloom, the ground colour should occupy three-quarters of the diameter from the edge of the centre or eye to the edge of the petals, the lacing occupying one quarter. Of the whole bloom, the tube and centre should occupy exactly half the diameter. Quite often the centre will be too large with the result that there will be insufficient ground colour. Or again, the ground colouring will occupy too large an area to the exclusion of the golden centre and edging, thus giving the bloom a dull appearance. Nor should there be any difference in colour between the centre and the lacing. If of very pale yellow or deep orange colouring, as the centre will sometimes be, this is a fault. Likewise where the ground colour is of a pale red colouring, a condition known to the old growers as 'foxy', the bloom will be unlikely to obtain commendation on the show bench. Sometimes the lacing will be found to be too thick and irregular and so will give the bloom a less rich appearance than where there is the correct amount of ground colour. Samuel Barlow has said that 'a first-class Gold Laced polyanthus will 'fetch' one at a glance by its brilliant appearance', and how right he was. There has yet to be raised the perfect bloom, but what fascination the Gold Laced polyanthus holds for its admirers both as an exhibition flower and in the garden.

The Royal Horticultural Society has suggested that ten points should be awarded for the perfect bloom and plant, divided as follows:—

Foliage and stem	...	...	...	1 Point
Truss ...	...	...	...	2 Points
Centre or eye ...	...	...	...	3 Points
Lacing ...	...	...	...	2 Points
Ground or body colour		...	...	2 Points

MERITS OF THE ORDINARY POLYANTHUS

The ordinary polyanthus is less exacting both in its culture and its definition. It is perhaps slightly hardier than the Gold Laced polyanthus, whilst there is not the same urgency to protect the blooms from rain and sunshine from which the Laced flowers may suffer if not protected. Nor is there so great a degree of accuracy in defining what constitutes a top class bloom. Those who grow the polyanthus for bedding or cutting could well enjoy the additional satisfaction to be obtained from exhibiting their most outstanding blooms.

Where plants in bloom are to be exhibited, the foliage should be healthy, clean and undamaged. The stems should be long, sturdy and erect so that the truss is held well above the foliage. The head or truss should be large, symmetrical and compact, though the blooms should not overlap. The often small, loosed truss of the older strains, where great gaps appeared between the pips made them quite unsuitable for the show bench. The pips should be of good size, substance and quite flat and they should be of a rich, bright colour. Blooms which have a thin, starry appearance and lack depth of colour should not be shown, neither should they be grown in the garden. It is suggested that twenty points are to be awarded for a top quality plant, divided as follows:—

Condition	5 Points
Stems	4 Points
Trusses	4 Points
Pips or blooms	4 Points
Colour	3 Points

Whilst the Gold Laced polyanthus, like the auricula, will almost always be exhibited with a single truss of bloom, the modern polyanthus is capable of bearing several, though perhaps two would be sufficient if bloom of outstanding quality is to be obtained.

There are numerous spring shows held each year during April and early May where one may exhibit the bloom or take notes of the truly magnificent polyanthus, primrose and auricula blooms to be seen exhibited each season. Enthusiasts would be well advised to join at least one of the National Primula and Auricula Societies, for there is a section catering for the Northern, Midland and Southern areas, and in addition there are the Royal Horticultural Society spring shows and various others to be held throughout the country. There is at least one show to be held in the vicinity of all polyanthus lovers who will be well rewarded by a visit.

10

THE POLYANTHUS IN WINDOW BOX AND TUB

Suitable strains and other plants for a spring display—Raising the plants—Making a Window box—Growing in Tubs—Pot culture.

DUE to their extreme hardiness and adaptability, the polyanthus is one of the best of all plants for a window box or tub. The plants will rarely be troubled by wind or rain, neither will snow or hard frost cause the foliage to be depleted, as so often happens with stocks and wallflowers, which bloom at the same time. Polyanthuses may be planted in any aspect; even a sunless position will not trouble them, though they will come later into bloom.

It will be advisable to use the bedding or shorter stemmed strains or varieties, and outstanding for window box culture are Lady Greer, Barrowby Gem and Beltany Red in the named varieties and any of the bedding strains, especially the Barnhaven Cowichan strain, Sutton's Fancy, and Blackmore and Langdon's Gold Medal strains. Each bears a compact truss of richest colouring on sturdy 10-inch stems. A few plants of Barrowby Gem should always be included, for it comes into bloom long before the end of winter and will continue until the others have finished flowering. It is delightful when planted with the brilliantly coloured Beltany Red.

The polyanthus is an ideal plant for a town house window box for the same reason that it is suitable for a town garden in that the foliage dies back and is untroubled by the sooty deposits of winter fogs. Varieties like Lady Greer and Beltany Red with their compact habit may also be planted with the more dainty spring flowering bulbs such as the muscari, crocuses, miniature daffodils and the small flowering species of the tulip. The bulb may be planted in the window box in groups of two or three around the polyanthus plants, setting them at the same time. Or the winter flowering pansies may be used to carpet the soil around the polyanthuses. Lovely flowering together is the winter flowering pansy March Beauty or Blue Boy with Barrowby Gem, or other yellow polyanthuses. Striking too, is Beltany Red and Blackmore and Langdon's Flame with white winter pansy, Snowstorm. Or plant the attractive grape hyacinth, Muscari Heavenly Blue, with a yellow polyanthus. By using the late winter flowering crocuses such as *C. chrysantha*, a window box may be made up with bulbs, pansies and polyanthuses to bloom on a sheltered wall from early February until the end of May when the box may be cleared and planted with the summer flowering plants such as geraniums or salvias.

RAISING THE PLANTS

The window box should be made up during late October, as soon as the summer flowering display has ended, and the plants may either be purchased each year, raised from seed, or lifted from the garden where they will have been planted after flowering and dividing. If kept moist through summer, and a shady border will prove ideal, the plants will have made considerable growth and will be sturdy and healthy when lifted for planting in the boxes at the end of autumn. Where there is no garden, but possibly only a small yard or verandah, the plants may still be grown on during summer by planting them in 9 to 10-inch deep boxes of soil well supplied with humus and protecting them from the sun. If kept well watered they will form sturdy plants by October. The bulbs, too, should be dried when the box is emptied and stored in a cool place until required for replanting in autumn. In this way, there is no reason why the polyanthus plants and bulbs should not last indefinitely.

Plants may be raised from seed by one of the methods described in a previous Chapter or, where there is no garden, seed may be sown in boxes or pans and covered with glass until germinated. A sunny window, courtyard, or verandah will be all that is necessary to raise the seedlings which should be transplanted into boxes when large enough to handle. The sowing compost should be that made up to the John Innes formula and is obtainable from any local seedsman or nursery, whilst the compost for growing on the plants should consist of sterilised loam to which peat, used hops, or leaf mould has been incorporated. A dozen plants will be sufficient for a window box of average size and so that they will bloom the first season, seed should be sown as early in spring as possible. For those who do not wish to raise their own plants, and this may be the only method of obtaining certain strains, plants may be obtained from a specialist grower when the boxes are being made up.

MAKING UP THE BOXES

Before placing any compost in the boxes it will be necessary to ensure thorough drainage. First the drainage holes in the base must be made so that the soil does not fall through, and this is best done by placing a piece of fine mesh wire netting over the base. Then add a layer of crocks to a depth of about $\frac{1}{2}$-inch to ensure efficient drainage during winter. Over the crocks, a layer of turves placed grass downwards will occupy another $1\frac{1}{2}$ inches of the box. The remaining space, depending upon the depth of the box, is filled with prepared compost.

The soil should preferably be taken from pasture, or be a good quality loam from a country garden and where the soil is not troubled by deposits of soot and sulphur. Soil taken from a town garden will generally be of an acid nature and will also contain a large number of weed seeds. Therefore pasture loam is greatly to be preferred. To this should be incorporated some peat or leaf mould, grit, or coarse sand to help with winter drainage, and a small quantity of decayed manure. The polyanthuses, bulbs and winter pansies will all appreciate a compost of this nature. A satisfactory compost will be obtained by mixing together

3 parts of loam
1 part peat or leaf mould
1 part sand or grit (by weight)
1 part decayed manure

A sprinkling of superphosphate of lime to encourage root action should be given and if the manure cannot be obtained, give 4 ozs. of bone meal to each box. The compost should be well drained during winter, but should contain sufficient humus to enable moisture to be retained during the often dry spring months, and this will reduce watering to a minimum. Should the loam be of a sandy nature, the grit or coarse sand may be omitted when mixing the compost. A sprinkling of lime or a few pieces of crushed charcoal should be added to the compost to maintain sweetness. Such a compost, whilst building up a vigorous, healthy plant will not require changing for at least two years.

Occupying the boxes for no more than six months, the plants may be set out quite closely together, allowing only 1 inch between them. Two rows of plants will be planted to the average sized box. Where inter-planting with bulbs, or with double daisies or winter flowering pansies, 2 inches should be allowed between the plants. The number of plants required will depend upon their size. When grown from an early spring sowing, almost half as many again will be required than where seed has been sown the previous autumn.

Plant firmly and water in, that being possibly all the watering necessary until the arrival of the warmer sun and the drier weather of spring, though where the boxes are situated on a shaded wall, facing north or east, almost no watering will be necessary throughout the life of the plants. When it is necessary to water the plants, always give a thorough soaking to enable the moisture to reach right down to the roots so that they do not turn upwards in search of it. However, on no account give so much water that it will soak through the soil and drip from the bottom of the box. Where the box is situated under the eaves of a house and against the wall where it will be shielded from the rains, it will tend to become dry even when the garden soil may be quite moist, so constant inspection of the compost should take place during the spring.

MAKING A WINDOW BOX

As window box gardening is now so popular, perhaps it will be of value to give some idea of how a box is made and erected. In making the box, and wood is the most suitable material, the exact measurements of the window must be taken so that the sides of the box will coincide with the framework of the window, the depth being in proportion to the depth of the window. The average sized window box will be 6-7 inches deep, 4 ft. long and 12-ins. wide, four bucketsful of compost being sufficient to fill it. A wooden box made of 1-inch timber, treated with preservative on the inside and painted on the outside to match the paintwork of the window frame, will prove long lasting and of pleasing appearance.

Strong timber will be required, for it must be remembered that a box filled with soil and plants has to carry a considerable weight. Timber for the front and back of the box should be cut to the lengths required, the ends fitting inside. When cutting the ends, allow for the thickness of wood so as to keep to the correct overall measurements required. If any attempt is made to dovetail the corners it should be remembered that the strength of a dovetail lies in the perfection of its construction and a water-resistant glue should be used. Always bear in mind that a good, simple job is better than a bad complicated one. When securing the two ends no advantage will be gained by using screws instead of 2-inch nails, for when driven in they only tend to part the grain, thus splitting the wood. For additional strength at the corners an angle bracket should be screwed either on the inside or outside of the box.

Adequate drainage holes should be made in the base, preferably making a dozen or so holes of $\frac{1}{2}$-inch diameter rather than half the number of 1-inch diameter, to ensure that there will be little of the compost escaping. Where possible always use hard wood, such as seasoned oak, in the construction of the box, or failing that, American Red Cedar, both of which will remain almost impervious to moisture through the years and neither of which require painting as a preservative.

After the box has been made up it should be treated on the inside with a wood preservative, Cuprinol being most efficient. This treatment is especially necessary if the box has been constructed of deal or other soft wood. Thoroughly soak the inside of the box and allow it to remain in the open after treating for at least ten days until it has become thoroughly weathered and any fumes which might be injurious to plant life, will have escaped. The box may then be painted on the outside only, to conform to one's tastes, or to the colour scheme of the house.

To make the container quite secure, the wall should be plugged with hardwood to a depth of not less than 2 inches, into which the brackets are screwed, or they may be fastened to the frame of the window itself. It is essential to see that there is no possible chance of the box protruding too far from the house, particularly where it is to overhang a public right of way, thereby causing injury to those who pass by, especially during hours of darkness. It is also equally important to ensure that neither the box nor its contents are able to fall on those below, otherwise the owner may find himself on the wrong side of the law. So before the box is filled and planted it must be fixed with the utmost care and a professional joiner should be called in for the purpose.

FIG. 2

It may be necessary, where birds are troublesome, to place black thread across the plants as soon as they come into bud. Where crocuses are being grown they will bloom early in spring and, if not protected, may also be damaged by birds.

GROWING IN TUBS

As an alternative to window box culture, the polyanthus may be enjoyed growing in tubs on a terrace, around a court-yard, or on a verandah. Allowing for a greater depth of soil than with a window box, a tub is an ideal method in which to grow the polyanthus with its liking for a deep, cool, moist soil. The plants will be especially useful for a shaded position, often caused by high walls or nearby property, and where little else would grow apart from certain bulbs. Muscari, snowdrops or iris reticulata planted around the tubs will provide added charm, or the more dwarf poly-anthuses or Juliae primroses may be planted around the outside of the tub, with the polyanthuses massed at the centre. In tubs the taller flowered strains may be used unless the situation is unduly exposed.

To enable the plants to take advantage of the greater depth of soil, the tubs must receive just the same thorough preparation as given the window box. In the same way, holes should be drilled at the base, over which is placed a layer of crocks or broken brick to a depth of 2 inches, so that in the event of wet weather, ample drainage is available. Over the crocks should be placed partially rooted turves and a layer of decayed stable manure. This should fill about half the tub. The rest of the tub should be filled with a similar compost as suggested for the plants where growing in a window box. Tubs possess another advantage over window boxes in that they do not require so much attention to watering. Being in a more open situation, they obtain natural moisture more easily, and possessing a greater depth of soil may be left unwatered for a longer period. A top dressing with peat after planting will also help to conserve moisture in the soil.

The most suitable tubs to use for planting are oak casks, sawn in two, which have been previously used for storing cider. They are of seasoned oak and will not require painting, though this may be done on the outside if the tubs are to be used round the whitewashed walls of a courtyard, or against the walls of a house. Old cider casks may be readily obtained at about half a guinea each from most West Country cider firms and will give years of service.

It should be said that before filling with soil, the tubs should be treated with a reliable wood preservative, both on the inside and outside and at least a fortnight should be allowed before the compost is added. To allow the soil to consolidate before planting, several days should be allowed after the tubs have been filled. If filled to the brim, this will allow the compost to settle down to about an inch below, which will allow for a summer top dressing and still prevent the soil from being splashed over the sides by heavy rains or watering. To prevent the soil from becoming sour it should be given a dressing of lime each autumn after the summer flowering plants have been removed. This, together with the greater depth of soil will make it unnecessary to remove and replace the soil as frequently as for window boxes. Every five years should be sufficient.

POT CULTURE

For a light, airy window, or for a porch, or a cold green-house, the polyanthus makes a most attractive pot plant, remaining in bloom for fully a month. The plants require no heat, indeed they will not tolerate any, and apart from an occasional watering they will require no other attention.

The most suitable plants will be unflowered seedlings

which were sown in July or August, transplanted in spring, and grown on in outdoor beds in partial shade until ready for lifting and potting the following March. The plants will, by then, have made large clumps and will send up a number of flower stems, coming into bloom several weeks earlier than where flowering in the open. Growing in pots in a cool place will prolong the polyanthus season by several weeks.

The plants should be lifted just as they commence to make new growth, early in March in the North, a fortnight earlier in the South. This will allow the plants time to become established before coming into bloom, though in an article appearing in the Journal of the Royal Horticultural Society in January 1956, Mr. Allan Langdon, V.M.H., of the famous Bath firm, wrote, 'lifting and potting can be done at any time . . . and I have seen plants lifted with buds showing, and which have made lovely pot plants, showing no signs of distress through having their roots disturbed'. This confirms the lines of John Clare in that the plants may be lifted when in full bloom, the cowslip and primrose behaving in the same way as the polyanthus.

The potting compost should consist of a friable loam, preferably from old pastureland, to which has been incorporated some moist peat or leaf mould and some decayed manure, preferably cow manure. Where this is unobtainable, a pinch of bone meal should be given to each 48 size pot. After the pots have been well crocked, the compost is added, the best method being to fill up the pots to about halfway, over which the roots are spread out. Additional soil is then packed around the roots and made quite firm. The plant is then well watered in.

Throughout their days in the pots, the plants should be shaded whenever the sun's rays become troublesome, whilst they should be given as much ventilation as necessary to maintain a buoyant atmosphere. The foliage should be syringed frequently, whilst an occasional application with diluted liquid manure will bring the flower trusses to perfection. Never, at any time, should the plants be grown in a stuffy atmosphere and they must never lack moisture.

Plants in pots may be taken into any cool room of the home, but so that the stems do not become 'drawn' it will be advisable to delay their moving until the buds begin to show colour. After flowering, the plants should be removed from the pots, divided, and replanted into a shaded bed outdoors.

The best strains for indoor blooming are those suggested for window box display and particularly the named varieties, Barrowby Gem and Hunter's Moon with their rich perfume, and the vivid Beltany Red. The Gold Laced polyanthus is an admirable plant for pot culture, this being the method by which it was generally grown in olden times.

11

PESTS AND DISEASES OF THE POLYANTHUS

Pests—Birds—Green fly—Primula aphis—Red spider—Slugs—Weevils —Wireworm—Diseases—Bread mould—Damping off—Root rot— Virus.

OF all hardy plants, the polyanthus is less troubled by pest and disease than almost any other plant. It is generally neglect which causes trouble and where the plants are given good cultivations from the beginning, neither pest nor disease should ever be experienced. All too often, however, the plants are grown in a dry soil, devoid of humus where they are exposed to the full rays of the summer sun. The result is that they lose vigour and quickly become a prey to numerous pests. Where the plants are kept in a vigorous, healthy condition, they will remain free of trouble for as long as it is desired to perpetuate the plants.

Pests

BIRDS. If they can be termed 'pests' the bird is the most troublesome of all polyanthus foes, removing the flower buds as they open and during dry periods, whole beds may be completely stripped of their flower buds within a few days. House sparrows and bullfinches are the worst culprits and where troublesome it will be necessary to place black thread across the beds just above the flowering stems. Alternatively, small pieces of tin fastened with string on to stakes about 2 ft. above ground level, so that they may jingle in the wind and so scare the birds away, will prove effective. It should not be thought that an odd bird appearing on the beds will cause no damage and although the plants themselves will not be harmed, they are quite capable of removing both buds and blooms, dropping them around the plants and leaving only the stems and untidy footstalks with nothing to show for twelve months labour. Birds should be looked upon as the most troublesome of all polyanthus foes whilst the plants are opening their blooms.

GREEN FLY. This member of the aphis family will occasionally prove troublesome to the polyanthus. It clusters on the foliage, generally around the neck, where it punctures the foliage and sucks out the sap causing the plants to lose vitality. The foliage first turns pale yellow, then becomes limp and less crinkled than normally, finally turning brown. This may be prevented by checking the pest before it obtains a hold, and fortunately eradication is an easy matter as the pest does not attack the plant below soil level. The pest may appear from the end of May, shortly after the plants have finished flowering, when they should be sprayed with Lindex solution or dusted with Lindex powder as for the Primula aphis. Take care to ensure that the liquid or dust reaches the crown and the neck of the plant just above soil level.

PRIMULA APHIS. Where the plants have been given either a soil which is too dry or one where excess winter moisture is unable to drain away, the plants will lose vitality and take on a sickly appearance. The first signs will be that the foliage will turn a pale yellowish-green colour, far removed from the rich, deep green foliage of the healthy plant. An unhealthy plant will quickly become infested by the Primula aphis, a pest which attacks all members of the family when given an opportunity. The greyish-white pests will be found clustering about the neck or crown of the plant, and if the plant is lifted they will also be found on the roots. The aphides will generally appear after the plants have finished flowering, during June, and will continue throughout the summer unless eradicated. They feed on the sap of the plant and quickly reduce its vigour. Where the attack is heavy the plant will die back completely.

Dry conditions would appear to be the chief cause and regular spraying of the plants during dry weather, and providing a mulch to maintain soil moisture should do much to prevent a serious outbreak. To allow the beds to become weed-infested will also encourage the pest, whilst any dead and decaying leaves and flower stems should be regularly removed as they form. Plants which may remain undivided longer than two years will also begin to lose vitality and be subject to attack.

Where the pest is observed, the plants should be sprayed with Lindex solution, taking care to reach the crown and around the neck. Use ½ fluid oz. to 2 gallons of water. This treatment should be repeated at fortnightly intervals until the trouble is cleared up, or longer should dry weather continue. An alternative method is to dust the plants with Lindex dust every ten days, taking care to reach the inside of the plant and the neck, where the pests generally congregate. Soaking the soil with Lindex solution around the plants will enable the insecticide to eradicate the pests below soil level.

If the pest is observed when the plants are being lifted and divided during mid-summer, or autumn, the plants should be washed, including the roots, in a soft soap solution, washing them again in clean water before replanting. Where the pests are seen densely congregating around the neck of a plant, it should first be brushed with methylated spirit, before being washed in soap solution and clean water. It will be advisable to treat any particularly valuable varieties or those bearing bloom of unusual colouring, in this way. D.D.T. dust should not be used for members of the primula family.

RED SPIDER. Polyanthus plants which are growing beneath a wall, in a shrubbery or in any position where the soil may tend to dry out frequently, and where the plants may be deprived of moisture on their foliage will be liable to an attack by red spider. Of this pest Maddock, the famous grower of Gold Laced polyanthuses of the mid-nineteenth century, said 'the worst enemy to the polyanthus is a small red or scarlet spider, which in summer spins its web on the underside of the leaves'. A century ago, the polyanthus was almost always cultivated in pots in a greenhouse, or similar structure, where the plants could be protected from adverse weather and they would therefore be more liable to attack from this pest. Plants growing outside except in the more sheltered and shaded positions will rarely be attacked, though it will be advisable to spray the plants regularly during a dry period, the red spider rarely appearing where the roots and foliage of the plants are kept moist. The secret of growing healthy polyanthus plants is never to allow them to lack moisture during spring and summer when the pest will be most troublesome. During dry periods, the plants should be sprayed with a hose or syringed where there are only small numbers, taking care to reach the underside of the foliage where the pests collect. The red spider cannot tolerate moisture and as it is a difficult pest to eradicate, when once it obtains a hold, and prevention being better than cure, make sure that the plants are always kept well supplied with moisture.

Where the leaves are to be seen turning brown, first at the edges, red spider should be diagnosed, although it is scarcely possible to observe the pest with the naked eye. The pests cluster underneath the leaves sucking the sap and undermining the vigour of the plant. Red spider will generally be most troublesome along the dry Eastern side of Britain, but plants growing almost anywhere may be attacked from early June until September where they lack moisture and during periods of drought. With red spider, prevention is always better than cure, but spraying with Dextrak Derris solution as for cucumbers, using $\frac{1}{2}$ fluid oz. to 2 gallons of water, will give some control.

SLUGS. These pests can be most troublesome to young plants occupying a frame or when planted out in beds, and particularly during a wet season. They may become so troublesome that they may quite easily devour a whole bed of seedlings in a night or two and so they should be protected as a matter of routine. Immediately the young plants have been set out, the ground (and plants) should be given a thorough soaking with Slugit, a slug exterminator in the liquid form which, unlike the solid forms, is neither harmful to human nor animal life. The treatment should be repeated every three weeks, and this should include tiny seedlings in boxes which are awaiting transplanting, as well as seedlings growing in a frame. As an additional precaution, the slugs may be removed from the beds or frames at nightfall with the aid of a torch. Everything possible should be done to keep the plants free from attack for otherwise the results of one's labours in crossing and raising new varieties, or where sowing the finest strains, would end only in failure. Nothing is more disappointing than where young plants of great vigour have been raised, only for them to be devoured by slugs.

WEEVILS. The root weevil is often a troublesome pest, the half-inch long, dark grey grubs being found beneath clumps of polyanthuses, which are generally in need of lifting and dividing. The presence of the larvae in the soil may be noticed by the plant failing to respond to spring conditions, new growth appearing slowly and finding difficulty in becoming established. If the plant is lifted, it will be found that the grubs have devoured many of the fleshy roots and occasionally almost nothing is to be found below soil level. Should the presence of the weevil be confirmed, Gammexane should be dusted over the roots before replanting, whilst the soil should also be given a light application, $\frac{1}{4}$ oz. per square yard. A too heavy application may cause stunted growth.

WIREWORM. In the old soil of town gardens, or in the newly dug garden, this pest may prove troublesome, attacking the plants below soil level and severing the roots. Should the attack be made before the plants have become well rooted, the plants may die back completely. Indeed, where wireworm is prevalent, serious damage may be done to a newly planted bed of polyanthus.

The old method of treating the ground with Naphthalene was reliable, but at least three weeks should elapse before any planting is done to enable the soil to rid itself of the undesirable fumes. A better method is to fork Lindex dust into the soil whilst the ground is being prepared, using 1 oz. per square yard. Or the soil may be given a thorough soaking with Lindex solution prior to planting should the ground already have been prepared. This could well be done as a matter of routine before any planting is done.

Diseases

BREAD MOULD. This is a disease of the seed which is more prevalent in America than in Britain. It is present as minute white specks on the seed and is often present where the seed has been harvested during a damp season. The disease becomes active upon sowing, the fungus attacking the newly germinated plant and causing it to die back almost before it has appeared above the soil. A preparation called Natriphene will kill the fungus if the seed is given a thorough soaking with the solution immediately after sown. It will also prevent damping off at a later stage.

DAMPING OFF. This is not the grey fungus which sometimes attacks auriculas and other members of the primula family growing indoors during the winter months, rather does it attack seedlings which are growing too closely together, the result of a too thick sowing. From the beginning, it is essential to allow the polyanthus a free circulation of air and whether the seed is sown in boxes or pans, or in a cold greenhouse, or frame, a too thick sowing should be guarded against. The seedlings will require an abundance of moisture and if this does not quickly dry off the tiny plants, the foliage will begin to damp off and soon the trouble will have spread to whole sections. Where this is observed, water less frequently, especially when the weather is damp or foggy, and give additional ventilation. Though the polyanthus enjoys a moist atmosphere, one which is stagnant must be avoided. The atmosphere for polyanthuses should always be sweet and buoyant. Where germinating the seed beneath a frame or in a greenhouse, care should be taken to see that water does not drip from the glass on to the young seedlings, for this will cause soil to splash on to the foliage, and will be almost sure to encourage damping off.

ROOT ROT. This trouble is caused by planting in badly drained soil, such as in a heavy soil which has not been opened up by humus or drainage materials, and though the polyanthus enjoys a considerable amount of moisture, stagnant moisture around the roots during the winter months may cause the fleshy roots to decay at the neck and the plant to perish. Prevention in this case, is the only means of protection.

VIRUS. Yellowing or blotching of the leaves and stunted growth may denote the presence of red spider or aphis, but it may also be caused by virus about which little is known and for which there is no known cure. If the plants do not respond to the treatment as advised for red spider and aphis, they should be dug up and burnt and the ground given a rest period when the remaining plants have finished blooming. Propagation should never be done with a virus infected plant. The disease may be introduced by aphides, which suck at the sap and so make it possible for the virus to enter the plant. It is therefore most important to keep the plants vigorous and free from aphis throughout their life. A plant attacked by pest will become weakly and lose vitality, and whether the virus is introduced in this way or not, a sickly plant will be more liable to succomb to disease.

INDEX